THE EBOOK REVOLUTION

THE EBOOK REVOLUTION

A Primer for Librarians on the Front Lines

Kate Sheehan

 LIBRARIES UNLIMITED

AN IMPRINT OF ABC-CLIO, LLC
Santa Barbara, California • Denver, Colorado • Oxford, England

Library of Congress Cataloging-in-Publication Data

Sheehan, Kate, 1978–
    The ebook revolution : a primer for librarians on the front lines / Kate Sheehan.
        pages cm
    Includes bibliographical references and index.
    ISBN 978–1–61069–183–3 (pbk.) — ISBN 978–1–61069–184–0 (ebook)
1. Libraries—Special collections—Electronic books. 2. Electronic books. 3. Libraries and electronic publishing. I. Title.
    Z692.E4S54   2013
    025.2'84—dc23   2012036186

ISBN: 978–1–61069–183–3
EISBN: 978–1–61069–184–0

17 16 15 14 13   1 2 3 4 5

This book is also available on the World Wide Web as an eBook.
Visit www.abc-clio.com for details.

Libraries Unlimited
An Imprint of ABC-CLIO, LLC

ABC-CLIO, LLC
130 Cremona Drive, P.O. Box 1911
Santa Barbara, California 93116-1911

This book is printed on acid-free paper ∞

Manufactured in the United States of America

Figures in Chapter 3 are reprinted with permission from Rainie, Lee, Kathryn Zickuhr, Kristen Purcell, Mary Madden, and Joanna Brenner, "The Rise of E-Reading," Pew Internet & American Life Project, April 4, 2012. Available online at http://libraries.pewinternet.org/2012/04/04/the-rise-of-e-reading/. Accessed December 6, 2012.

CONTENTS

ACKNOWLEDGMENTS

A very large number of people have been kind and helpful as I've worked on this project. I'm terribly afraid I'll miss someone, but will do my utmost to be complete. Since this book has coincided with pregnancy, a number of people have asked me to compare the two. I'm not sure that's possible, but I will say that both book and baby (even a short book with a limited audience and a relatively easy pregnancy) bring out people's generosity and have a general restore-your-faith-in-humanity effect.

Many thanks to Linda Braun and Sarah Ludwig who put me in touch with the wonderful Barbara Ittner at Libraries Unlimited (should anyone doubt the value of publishing, editors like Barbara make the whole business worthwhile) and encouraged me to submit my original book proposal. Sarah also let me drink all of her coffee while she read my proposal and made excellent suggestions for improvement.

An astonishing group of book people spoke to me about their jobs and the book ecosystem. I learned huge amounts from Ruth Liebmann, Michael Porter, Mike Shatzkin, Jess Johns, Jamie LaRue, Monique Sendze, Andromeda Yelton, Juliet Grames, Bronwen Hruska, Eric Hansen, Steve Cauffman, Kendall Wiggin, Dan Suchy, and Molly Raphael. Lee Rainie of the Pew Research Center's Internet & American Life Project was kind enough to let me look at some of the data ahead of publication so that I could meet my own publication deadline. He's long been a friend to libraries, and I am grateful for the chance to include more up-to-date information as well as the great work Pew has done in providing all of us with nonpartisan data and reports. Pew was also generous in letting me use their charts, including re-creating them with the resolution needed for print publication.

My coworkers have been enormously patient about and supportive of my second job. Mike Simonds, Amy Terlaga, Tom Sweda, Melissa Lefebvre, Carol Yarrison, Jessica Venturo, Ben Shum, Gen Francis, Jenn Clark, Ted Mackewitz, Mary Llewellyn, Steven Pisani, Robin Fitch, Nancy Mazer, and Joan Shamatovich at Bibliomation headquarters have all listened to me complain and cheered me on. Amy and Jessica in particular have had to put up with the fact that even though I've been eating, sleeping, and breathing eBooks, I still have to check with them on half the OverDrive support requests I attempt to answer.

Christopher Platt and Heather McCormack very kindly suggested me as a panelist at Digital Book World 2012, which was a fantastic experience, and I am forever in their debt for putting my name on the table. Heather let me follow her around the conference, introducing me to a million people and the best donut I have ever had.

The Connecticut Ebook Task Force, led by Ernie DiMattia, has been a wonderful group to work and talk eBooks with and they've let me piggyback on our work, using vendor presentations and interviews with librarians to ask a million questions and take notes that have ended up in these pages. Their indulgence has been much appreciated.

Similarly, Patrick Hogan at ALA TechSource asked me to cover Tools of Change and I happily agreed. As with Digital Book World, the exposure to a publishing conference was enlightening and has informed much of my work on this book. I'm grateful for the opportunity to write about the conference and the chance to learn more about publishing.

Karen Schneider (known to my family as my library fairy godmother) and Brett Bonfield have both talked about eBooks with me and helped clarify a lot of my thinking. They also spent a weekend workshopping an essay about HarperCollins and OverDrive for *Publishers Weekly* that led to this book. I owe them both a lifetime supply of oatmeal.

Librarians are wonderful people, and I have been lucky to have some fantastic colleagues and friends. Librarians from Bibliomation's libraries have discussed eBooks with me at countless meetings and let me pick their brains about what they'd like to know more about. Connecticut's abundance of fabulous librarians has been a boon to me. Rebecca Stine, Jaime Hammond, Lisa Carlucci Thomas, Merry Uk, Abby Sesselberg, Gretchen Caserotti, John Blyberg, Jill Dugas Hughes, Ramona Harten, Debbie Herman, and Sharon Brettschneider have all been willing eBook discussion partners, and I can't believe so much talent is crammed into this small state. There are, of course, wonderful librarians everywhere, and Jason Griffey, Cindi Trainor, Kathryn Greenhill, Barbara Genco, and Josh Hadro have all let me bounce ideas off of them and offered helpful feedback. I'd be remiss if I didn't mention Twitter and all of the librarians, writers, and publishing types there. They've been great fun to talk shop with. It's surprising what you can learn in 140-character bursts.

Of course, my family and friends have put up with a lot of book- and baby-talk, stress, and general obsessiveness. My lovely and supportive parents, Jeanne and Kevin Sheehan; my sibling-in-laws (I can't believe I lucked into this family) Adrienne and Ron Conti, Mark and Joanne Giannelli, and Glen and Patti Giannelli; and my nearest and dearest (and surprisingly nonlibrarian) friends, Louisa Pyle and Laura Lamp, have all made the last several months bearable. Most importantly, Gary Giannelli, my amazing husband who has put up with my nights and weekends (and our dinner table conversation) being consumed by eBooks, research, and writing and who has been stuck with the vast majority of domestic chores, including new and daunting tasks like assembling baby gear. You're astounding and I can't wait to cross this next threshold with you.

INTRODUCTION

eBooks. Did you just sigh? I've noticed that librarians sigh heavily when eBooks come up. Most of the public and school librarians I interact with want to know more about eBooks and wish they had time to do more research on all things eBook. In the meantime, they have enormous patron demand, shrinking budgets, and a library to run. Not to mention the inevitable "eBooks are destroying libraries" conversations with friends, relatives, and anyone else who finds out you're a librarian (we've all had the eBook chat with our doctors, right? Nothing says "I want to talk about the demise of my profession" like a paper gown).

Everybody knows something about eBooks, but nobody feels like they know enough. In any group of librarians, I've found that most will profess confusion and a feeling of being underinformed about eBooks, yet the group often knows more than they realize. eBooks can be an emotional subject for many of us (see the "demise of my profession" conversation above). Like most librarians, I knew that I should know more about eBooks, and I followed my colleagues who seemed to be on top of things, but I never felt like I knew enough. The decision by HarperCollins to limit library eBooks to 26 circulations was a watershed moment for me. I realized that I had been assuming that the status quo would prevail and that at some point, other publishers would work with libraries. Unconscious entitlement had made me lazy, thinking that publishers would have to come around, because libraries have always been here and always will be here.

The more I dug into eBooks, the more overwhelming it all seemed—the sense of trying to drink from a fire hose exacerbated by my newfound sense of urgency. Most days, I was glad that this was a professional side interest, not my main job. Still thinking of eBooks as a minor interest, I approached Libraries Unlimited looking to write an entirely different book. A few conversations with editor Barbara Ittner later and I was writing a proposal for a book on eBooks. Once eBooks went from being a casual professional dalliance to a part-time job, the fire hose actually became harder to manage in many ways. Every day things are changing; new data, new publishers, and new perspectives emerge hourly. Keeping up with every aspect of all things eBook is a full-time job (and then some). I've been reading everything I can about eBooks for the past several months, and it's shown me how many things I don't know and how many books, articles, and blog posts I'll never be able to get to. And then a publisher or tech company or bookseller makes a major announcement and everything is different again. A friend suggested I just stop writing at some point, leave several blank pages, and say that things are changing too fast, so you can write your own ending here. Blank pages or no, that's what's going to happen—much of the content here will be different by the time you're holding this book in your hands (or looking at it on your eReader) and the ending will be something entirely new.

As I've worked on this project, I've tried to keep my colleagues in mind. I work for a consortium of public and school libraries in Connecticut. Every one of our librarians is strapped for time. Their budgets are lean, their staffing is bare-bones, and their door counts are huge. Any one of the topics in this book could merit a book on its own, but I've tried to boil it down to the essentials (read: short sections you can read while you're trying to do two other things) and give the reader an overview of the eBook ecosystem. It's easy to get caught up in library vendors and practices, and those are things that librarians are good at learning about. There are already excellent resources available for someone who wants to pick an eBook vendor or pilot an eReader lending program. I've touched on those topics, but spent the most time on the things I hear librarians ask about: the nuts and bolts of eBooks, how publishers view eBooks, and the impact of Amazon. eBooks are evolving inside and outside of libraries, and I've spent more time looking at the eBook world outside of libraries. Right now, publishers and companies like Amazon and Apple hold far more power than libraries or library vendors. That's always been the case, but with eBooks, the constant state of change makes that power imbalance all the more noticeable. I'm not trying to suggest or encourage any animosity between libraries and other eBook stakeholders, but we have very different goals and needs. As we feel our way through the eBook revolution, advocacy for library interests will be critical.

This book is not intended to be comprehensive, and I'm aware of the irony of publishing a print book about eBooks. Even if you're reading this as an eBook, it still went through the traditional publishing process. I wrote most of it in late 2011 and early 2012 with revisions in the spring of 2012 and a few small revisions in July and September 2012, so it will be automatically out of date by the time it gets into your hands. To keep it as useful as possible, it's intended as a primer to the big-picture issues around eBooks. My own background is in public libraries and that's my primary audience. If you've been following eBook news avidly, I hope you'll find some new resources and perspectives here. If you've been feeling like you're too busy to do anything about eBooks, I hope this is the book for you. You can read it straight through or dip in and out of sections. I've tried to keep the paragraphs and sections short, as is the convention online, because I imagine a harried colleague paging through this while she tries to eat her sandwich in peace. This is not a buying guide or complete education on digital content. There are bullet lists of suggestions, guidelines, and resources throughout the book. I took the word "primer" seriously and tried to cover the basics of both eBooks generally and eBooks in libraries. I hope you find this book useful. There is also a companion site, ebookprimer.com, where I will post updates to the content here, and eBook and publishing news that affects libraries.

CHAPTER 1

eBook Basics

THE SCENT OF AN EBOOK

Any discussion about books, libraries, and eBooks will inevitably include at least one comment (usually several comments) about the scent of a book, the feel of paper, or the heft of a printed tome. These are all wonderful and lovely things, to be sure, but they're not going to derail the cultural and technological shift before us. Horses smell better than cars, and gorgeous wooden radios feel nicer than plasma-screen televisions, but sensory experiences aren't completely driving our information consumption decisions. Print is not dead. As Eli Neiburger says, books aren't obsolete, they're outmoded (Neiburger 2011b).

Personally, I'm still buying, borrowing, and using a lot of print books. Most of the books I've cited in these pages are books that I have paper copies of. But there's no denying the centrality of the screen in most of our lives. Although I still favor paper books, I do most of my reading on screens. Librarians are besieged with requests for eBooks daily. We may get a little glassy-eyed when we inhale deeply in a used-book store, but even if you loathe eReaders, there's no denying their growing popularity. Print is by no means dead. As many people writing about eBooks and technology have observed, the radio was not replaced by the television. While it's tempting to liken the rise of eBooks to the shift from tapes to CDs, the radio/television metaphor may be more apt. Different people will prefer different formats, and eBooks will evolve capabilities that print can't match. Conversely, print will doubtless be preferred for certain types of books or information.

The first eBook was born out of Michael Hart's vision of what the Internet would become. In 1971, Hart typed the Declaration of Independence into a mainframe and shared it with a few other people, giving birth to what would eventually be known as Project Gutenberg. Since that time, the humble electronic text has become tremendously more complicated. File format, digital rights management (DRM), hardware, and licensing all play crucial roles in how we consume eBooks.

EBOOK HARDWARE

Hardware is the area of the eBook world that is the easiest to talk about at cocktail parties. File formats and DRM (the software that stops readers from easily sharing eBooks—more on that later) just don't have the cachet of a shiny new gadget. As with file formats, there are a lot of eBook readers out there, but only a few dominate the market, so we'll focus on those here.

Your Computer

It's been possible to read eBooks on your computer since the first time you sat down in front of a monitor and keyboard. Depending on the file type and DRM, you may have to open your eBook in specific software, but computers have always been eBook-friendly hardware. Their portability leaves something to be desired—reading on a laptop screen while waiting in line at the grocery store doesn't work for most of us, but they're familiar and many people already own them. You can easily open a PDF or text file on your computer or you can use eBook reader software found online or provided by most eBook vendors.

Your Smartphone

Like your computer, your smartphone has always been capable of storing and displaying eBooks. Even those early (now terribly clunky) Palm Pilots could display eBooks (that was Mobipocket's original market). More recent smartphones have access to apps for eBooks and apps that are eBooks. Reading on a phone may strain the eyes, but is probably more gratifying than checking eMail while you're in a checkout line.

Kindle

Although there were eBook readers available well before the Kindle, Amazon's device was groundbreaking. The Kindle was released in 2007, and Oprah declared it one of her "favorite things" in 2008. The Kindle is the most popular eReader on the market. The screen of the original Kindle employs E Ink technology that, unlike a computer screen, is not backlit. E Ink can be read in direct sunlight and is perceived as being easier on the eyes (though newer LCD screens are not as tiring to use as older backlit screens) (Bolton 2010). However, E Ink is currently available only in black-and-white. The year 2011 saw the release of the Kindle Fire, an LCD tablet from Amazon. The Fire has a color screen and can be used to watch movies and television shows, and browse the web. In September 2012, Amazon revised the entire Kindle line, phasing out the larger-screen DX and the Kindle Touch, and introducing the Paperwhite, a Kindle with a new front-lit screen. Amazon also gave the Paperwhite an improved battery life, making it the flagship of the Kindle eReader devices. The company also expanded the Kindle Fire devices to include high definition (HD) versions, one with a seven-inch display and two with 8.9-inch displays. The most expensive version includes 4G connectivity, which means it can connect to the internet using either wifi or AT&T's cellular network. The Kindle, Kindle Paperwhite, and Kindle Keyboard all have two price points: one with "special offers" and one without. The "special offers" are ads that play on the device's screen saver and appear on the bottom of the home screen. The new Kindle Fire line originally did not have the option to remove the special offers, but Amazon responded to complaints by allowing Fire HD owners to pay $15 to opt-out of the ads (Biggs 2012). However, "special offers" is listed as feature of the Fire line of Kindles. Amazon's sales figures are closely guarded, but one estimate has 5.5 million Kindle Fires being sold in the 2011 holiday season.

The device allowed Amazon to move from selling books to publishing them. Amazon produces both eBooks and Kindle Singles, which are shorter works, written expressly for Kindle users. Authors can self-publish through Amazon's Kindle store, blurring the lines between bookseller, publisher, and technology company.

Nook

Barnes & Noble's eReader, like the Kindle, limits its user to the inventory of the bookseller who produces it. Unlike Amazon, Barnes & Noble does not offer a self-publishing component to their eBook business. Barnes & Noble does make the Nook in both E Ink and color. The color Nook is built on the Android platform, and Barnes & Noble offers apps and web browsing on the device. Magazines are also popular on the color Nook, as the screen displays the content more faithfully than E Ink can. In 2011, Barnes & Noble released the Nook Tablet, which, like the Amazon Fire, is designed to be a media consumption device, with apps for movie and television viewing preinstalled. The Nook Color has many of the same tablet features, though the apps for movie and television streaming are not preinstalled. The other Nook is the Nook SimpleTouch, an E Ink reader with a touch screen. Barnes & Noble released the Nook SimpleTouch with GlowLight in the spring of 2012, an E Ink reader with a built-in front light that allows the reader to see the E Ink screen in dim lighting, prompting David Pogue to say "there's no better E Ink model than this new glowing Nook" (Pogue 2012). In 2012, Barnes & Noble announced that the Nook SimpleTouch would be free and the Nook Color would be $99 (half its original cost), with a one-year subscription to the *New York Times* on the devices. This was announced as a promotion, and a PaidContent.org story reported there would be a similar arrangement for subscribers to *People Magazine*, with Time, Inc. (*People Magazine*'s publisher) splitting the cost of the discounted Nooks with Barnes & Noble (Owen 2012a). There were also rumors in early 2012 that Barnes & Noble was considering spinning the Nook business off into a separate company. In April of 2012, Microsoft and Barnes & Noble formed an alliance (even though Microsoft was suing Barnes & Noble over the Nook a year earlier), with Microsoft investing $300 million in a new subsidiary company. Barnes & Noble will own 82.4 percent of the new company, and Microsoft will own 17.6 percent. The new company will include both Barnes & Noble's digital and college businesses (Smith 2012).

iPad/Tablets

The iPad is not strictly an eReader, but a tablet computer. However, with the iPad came the advent of the iBook store. The iPad has also given rise to book apps. T. S. Eliot's "The Waste Land," despite the fact that "a $14 version of a famously enigmatic early 20th-century poem written by a decidedly unsexy dead guy—and in the public domain, no less!—would hardly seem the sort of thing to become a hit in the iTunes app store" (L. Miller 2011), made a surprising splash when it was released in app form. Although the iPad is the dominant tablet on the market right now, other tablet computers are eBook friendly. Android tablets are manufactured by a variety of companies and run the Android operating system, an open-source system that runs on tablets and phones. In 2011, iPad had 57.6 percent of the global tablet market and Android had 39.1 percent, a 10 percent increase over 2010 due in large part to the Kindle Fire and Barnes & Noble tablet (M. Miller 2011).

Sony

Sony's eReader is near and dear to many a librarian's heart. The original Sony eReader came out in 2006, and by 2009 Sony had partnered with Overdrive to make library eBooks available to owners of the device (Patel 2009). There have been several generations of the Sony eReader, but in 2011 Sony released a single reader and discontinued all of their previous models. The Reader Wi-Fi is a black-and-white E Ink touch-screen device. Sony books have their own file format, BBeB Book (LRF), but the eReader will also display ePub, PDFs (portable document format), and plain text. They've been trailing behind Kindles and Nooks in the eReader market, but Digital Book World predicts a possible resurgence for Sony in 2012 with the launch of Pottermore, the Harry Potter eBook platform (Greenfield 2011b).

Kobo

Kobo launched at the CTIA trade show, a technology show with an emphasis on wireless devices, in 2010. Initially, the eReader was sold by Borders, though Kobo prided itself on interoperability, releasing a "Powered by Kobo" application for iPhone/iPad, BlackBerry, Palm Pre, and Android phones at the same time as their first eReader (Hambien 2010). Kobo was a spin-off of Indigo Books & Music, a large Canadian chain of bookstores, and Indigo remains a major investor in the company (Sapieha 2012). Kobo's line of eReaders includes the Kobo Mini (a five-inch touchscreen E Ink reader), the Kobo Touch (a six-inch touch-screen eReader available with or without offers), the Kobo Glo (a six-inch touch-screen E Ink reader with a built-in front light), and the Kobo Arc (a seven-inch color tablet). Kobo sells its devices across the world, and the 2011 holiday season proved to be a strong one for the company, with a 10-fold increase in Kobo ownership from their preholiday numbers (Biba 2012). Following in Amazon's footsteps, Kobo plans to launch a publishing division in 2012 (Pilkington 2011).

Gadgets in Your Library

Kindles and iPads rule the marketplace. It's easy to scoff at the idea of reading an entire novel on a phone, but smartphones are getting larger and users are getting accustomed to reading on handheld devices. If you're thinking of buying gadgets for your library staff to practice on, the most popular devices are always going to be safe bets. If the cost of an iPad is too high, consider asking staff with iPhones or iPads to show their colleagues how to access eBooks on them. Although there are some differences between iPads, iPhones, and iPod Touches, the basic principles of use are similar. They can also serve double duty as devices for roaming reference. For the best library gadget insight, I recommend Jason Griffey's blog, workshops, and publications. His main blog can be found here—http://jasongriffey.net/wp/—and he writes about gadgets for ALA TechSource regularly: http://www.alatechsource.org/blogger/16.

FILE FORMATS

When you save a document in Microsoft Word, your computer appends a file type to your document name. You click "Save As," christen your document "The Great American Novel," and Word adds ".doc" or ".docx" to the end. Similarly, when you buy music online (I'll assume that my readers are purchasing instead of pirating their songs), you may seek out Mp3s or AAC files. These are different types of file formats, and like all digital content, eBooks come in a myriad of formats.

Right now, file formats seem to be inextricably linked to readers, but that is slowly changing. When personal computers (PCs) were still a novelty, files created on Macintosh computers could not be read on PCs (then often called IBM-compatible machines) and vice versa. A document written in Microsoft Word couldn't be opened by MacWrite. Today, those once-impossible barriers are relatively inconsequential. eBooks are still in their infancy, and file formats are important apart from their associated hardware.

There are a tremendous number of eBook formats, but for simplicity's sake, we'll focus on the most popular here. There are other formats on the wane, like Sony's BroadBand eBook (BBeB), which the company is phasing out in favor of ePub. ("eBook formats" eBook Architects). You may also encounter some formats that aren't really formats, like Smashwords, which is an eBook distributor that allows anyone to upload a Microsoft Word file, which the site then converts into 10 different formats ("eBook formats" eBook Architects).

Amazon (.azw, .mobi)

In 2005, Amazon purchased Mobipocket, a company devoted to eBook reading on mobile devices ("About Mobipocket"). Amazon developed the Mobipocket format into the .azw format for the Kindle. It can be read on the Amazon Kindle and Kindle apps. In 2011, Amazon announced the Kindle Format 8 (KF8), which replaced the previous format, called Mobi 7. Amazon also informed publishers that they would begin the process of shutting down Mobipocket in late 2011 (Hoffelder 2011). KF8 supports HTML and CSS, including the ability to specify a downloadable font, create animation, incorporate sounds, and let text flow around high-quality graphics (Shankland 2011). Amazon offers information and publisher tools for working with their format at http://www.amazon.com/gp/feature.html?docId=1000729511

ePub (.epub)

The ePub format is the digital publishing standard of the International Digital Publishing Forum, a nonprofit organization made up of publishing and technology companies (International Digital Publishing Forum "Epub"). It can be read on most eReaders, with the notable exception of the Amazon Kindle. ePub3 is the newest release of the ePub standard. It includes specifications for web content, such as HTML 5, CSS, images, audio, and video. It also includes media overlays, which allow for the synchronization of text and audio (International Digital Publishing Forum "Epub3 Overview"). As this standard is more widely used and its features exploited, we will likely see eBooks that are more like apps and less like printed books. eBooks already have games, customized calculators (in diet and exercise books, for example), and interactivity built in. ePub3 will allow for an expansion of these types of features, and authors will begin writing with that in mind.

At Digital Book World 2012, there was a panel discussion on ePub3 that I found enlightening. The move to ePub3, while much touted, is not as smooth as those of us outside the publishing business might assume. Peter Balis, director, digital business development at John Wiley & Sons, said that digital-content providers want to "coalesce around ePub3," and while the rest of the panelists agreed, they were concerned about some limitations in the new format specification. Specifically, the conversation focused on reflowable versus fixed layouts. For most straight text, reflowable is fine and doesn't alter the content of the book in any way. Readers can change the font or the size of the text, and read on large computer screens or tiny cell phone screens. Reflowable eBooks allow for all of that. ePub3 actively discourages fixed layouts and does not provide technical specifications for achieving fixed layouts. When publishers want to create eBooks for books that benefit from a fixed layout, like many children's books, craft books, graphic novels, manga, cookbooks, poetry, and, in the case of Simon & Schuster, the Folger Shakespeare Library, they are left with creating a separate product for each eBook reader. The panelists discussed the limitations of this process, not least of which is the increased workload and reduced ability to automate processes to produce one title as an eBook for multiple platforms. Should each version have its own ISBN? If one platform can support certain enhancements, and another platform can support different enhancements, is calling an eBook "enhanced" meaningful to consumers? A set of best practices for ePub3 and fixed layout was mentioned as a solution, though the difficulties of forging agreement between retailers and publishers are not insignificant.

PDF (.pdf)

PDF is a file format created by Adobe. PDFs can be viewed on almost any computer, eReader, or mobile device. However, PDFs are intended to preserve formatting, making them less easy to read on smaller screens, such as those on phones and eReaders ("eBook formats" eBook Architects).

XPS (.xps)

The XML Paper Specification (XPS) is Microsoft's alternative to the PDF (Windows Dev Center). Baker and Taylor's Blio platform uses XPS files.

OTHER FORMATS

eBooks can also be published in HTML, plain text, or a wide range of proprietary formats associated with specific readers. Librarians familiar with Project Gutenberg have likely seen the list of available eBook formats there, which includes both HTML and plain text.

Apple announced their entry into the textbook-publishing business with iBooks2 and iBooks Author. The iBooks 2.0 format is a modification of the ePub standard (Bjarnason 2012), with proprietary elements (largely CSS components) that prevent iBooks 2 files from being read by standard ePub readers (Glazman 2012). This shift away from the open standard surprised many, and the ramifications of another file format remain to be seen (Bott 2012).

Are your eyes crossed yet?

The seeming free-for-all in eBook formats can be confusing. Just to add a little more confusion to the mix, there is software called Calibre that can convert files from one type of eBook format to another. However, it does not work on copyrighted material. It is possible to download plug-ins for Calibre that will illegally convert newer titles and allow a book purchased on a Kindle to be read on a Nook. If the comments on David Pogue's post about these plug-ins and other eBook reader compatibility issues (http://pogue.blogs.nytimes.com/2012/05/10/how-compatible-are-rival-e-readers/) are any indication, many people don't understand that it's illegal to do so. Their confusion is understandable: buying a book from Amazon doesn't prevent a reader from taking that book into a Barnes & Noble to read, but eBooks are not the same as physical books. Fortunately, mainstream tech writers like Pogue write about these issues regularly and can be used as a double check when your instincts are telling you that this super software your patron is enthusing about does not belong on library computers.

eReader and tablet reviews are everywhere online, and you likely already have a favorite review source. David Pogue writes frequently about eReaders and tablets for the *New York Times*, and sites like CNET include reviews of eReaders and tablets. The Pew Internet and American Life Project is an excellent place to get statistics on device ownership and use (http://pewinternet.org/).

A NOTE ON TABLETS VERSUS EREADERS

Although the iPad is the dominant tablet on the market at this time, and the Kindle and Nook are the two most prominent eReaders, there are a variety of devices available. Sony's eReader has been popular with libraries, since it too could use library eBooks. Other eReader devices do exist, and many accept library eBooks. Android tablets abound as well. The eReader may be a transitional device, with multiuse tablets taking precedence in the long term, but right now librarians are likely to see both tablets and eReaders cross their desk.

All three major commercial vendors—Amazon, Apple, and Barnes & Noble—have the same thing in common: they sell a piece of hardware that locks the consumer in to buying content from the same company. There are ways around this, of course. Apple's app store offers a variety of book-related apps, including those for the Kindle and the Nook. It's therefore possible to buy an iPad and read books from a variety of vendors on it. The Nook Color can be turned into a tablet device using the Android operating system, either through "rooting," which overwrites the Nook's software, or through a micro SD card with the Android system installed, creating a dual-boot device. Both Amazon and Barnes & Noble have gotten into the tablet business, which makes sense, as consumers are looking for multiuse devices, and both companies can sell a wider variety of media to owners of their tablets.

Devices sold by the same companies that sell content for those devices are going to optimize the process for purchasing content from that company. People who buy Kindles are likely to buy almost all of the content for that device from Amazon, and people who buy Nooks are going to shop at Barnes & Noble. There are companies devoted entirely to making accessories for handheld devices. But once a reader purchases an eReader, they are largely committed to purchasing all of their books from that same company. Moving from one company to another is as onerous a shift as moving from Mac to PC was 15 years ago. As publishers consider dropping DRM, that may be changing.

IS AN EBOOK A BOOK?

Underpinning much of the conversation about eBooks is the persistent question: is an eBook a book? It's tempting to compare eBooks to their predecessors in the move to digital media. Mp3s changed how we purchase and consume music—musicians still make albums, but we can cherry-pick the bits we like, buying only the upbeat Lady Gaga songs we like to listen to while we exercise and ignoring her ballads. eBooks aren't yet producing a wave of chapter purchasing, although ventures like Byliner, Kindle Singles, and Random House's Brain Shots are drawing attention to medium-length work, and publishers are interested in selling sections of longer-form nonfiction as stand-alone eBooks. Right now, for the most part, an eBook is a digital version of the thing we'd get in print.

Except when it's not. eBooks don't come with the right of first sale, making library loaning a bit more complicated. Private loaning is also curtailed. Amazon and Barnes & Noble both allow a limited sort of loan from their eReaders. eBooks can be loaned only once, and that loan is restricted to owners of the same kind of device it was loaned from. A Kindle book cannot be loaned to a Nook, and vice versa. Librarians fielding requests to accept donated eBooks have to explain that eBooks are very much not like books in this regard.

When we do loan eBooks, we loan them as if they are paper, which simultaneously makes perfect sense and none at all. There are eBooks that can be loaned to multiple users. Anything in the public domain is freely or cheaply available through many eBook vendors and on Project Gutenberg. Library vendors do offer the option to allow multiple users for certain titles, particularly in the school and academic markets. The pricing structure for those eBooks is usually different, and simultaneous use isn't available for all titles, but it is possible.

Loaning library eBooks as if they are books certainly makes sense from a publisher's point of view. If a library could buy one copy of a book and loan it out to everyone who was interested in it at once, there wouldn't be any incentive to buy a second copy of that book, decreasing libraries' value to publishers. It makes less sense to patrons who wonder why the library doesn't understand how computer files work. For librarians, long hold lines or difficulty with course reserves makes the paperness of eBooks frustrating, but budget restrictions may make us wary of a multiuse license.

Budget concerns are pervasive in the eBook discussion. eBooks are popular with libraries that buy them, eating up more and more of diminishing book budgets. At first glance, eBooks seem like just another format to buy. Libraries already buy books in paper, on CD, and in large print, so why not as an eBook, too? However, eBooks are in much higher demand than audiobooks or large print, and they are widely seen as a potential replacement for print. eBooks are also instantaneous; patrons who may have merely grumbled about waiting on a long hold list for a print book find such waiting intolerable when they can buy an eBook in seconds.

eBooks are also available to only a small, privileged percentage of the population. The equalizing power of the library is taken out of play with eBooks. They are not for everyone. The additional cost of providing eBooks is not feasible for every library. For many libraries, the only way to offer eBooks is through a consortial purchasing arrangement. Shared collections offer a lower bar for entry, and because they are shared, they partially offset the inability to loan individual titles between libraries, though they usually come with longer wait times for popular titles and the looming threat of publisher mistrust of shared collections. Still, the issue of eReader ownership remains. Even if eReaders are free, they require both literacy and some technical knowledge to use. Children who grow up around books have been found to be more successful (National Endowment for the Arts [NEA] 2007, 71–74), possibly because once they can read, they can pick up any of the volumes in their home. eReaders potentially present a greater barrier to use.

We have ceased to think of books as a technology, but they are an information device in their own right. Several years ago, librarians were sending around a YouTube clip of a comedy sketch that depicted a medieval monastery IT person showing a monk how to use a book. While the video was meant in jest, the codex has not always reigned supreme. The earliest libraries were collections of clay tablets. Unlike the papyrus scrolls that supplanted them, these tablets were durable and less likely to be lost in a library fire. "These durable books of clay lent themselves to the library-building impulse; as early as the third millennium B.C., a temple at the town of Nippur, in what is now southeastern Iraq, included archive rooms filled with tablets" (Battles 2003, 25). The library at Alexandria was, of course, filled with loosely organized papyrus scrolls (Battles 2003, 28). The Roman wax tablet gave rise to the codex we know today, with the book becoming prevalent in the fifth century CE (Chin 2006).

Touch screens have certainly made eReaders and tablets more intuitive. Children now expect all screens to respond to touch. In a 2008 talk at the Web 2.0 Expo, Clay Shirky told a story about a child rooting around behind the television, looking for the mouse. She couldn't imagine media she couldn't interact with. In 2012, that child would be poking the screen, wondering why she couldn't change the channel or interact with the story. As Shirky put it, "Here's what four-year olds know: a screen that ships without a mouse ships broken." A few years later, and four-year-olds are tapping their television screens, thinking that machines that don't respond to touch are broken.

Interactivity is a much-touted advancement that eBooks provide. The Kindle Fire, Nook Tablet, and iPad all boast books with video clips, interactive animations, and other features impossible with the printed page. Blio eReading software includes sound effects and built-in dictionaries, and can read to the blind or highlight words as it reads aloud to children. How much interactivity contributes to traditional literacy remains to be seen, but practitioners of the growing field of transliteracy argue that this new skill set—interaction and content creation across a variety of platforms—is crucial for twenty-first-century learners.

By taking a text and making it digital, are we fundamentally transforming what it is? When we add sounds, location awareness, and interactivity, the book has clearly become something different. But is a digital copy of something on an eReader fundamentally different from those same words in a codex? For the reader, maybe not, at least some of the time. A great story will pull the reader in, regardless of format. Text is our primary method of cultural communication, on a page or on a screen. But we do treat a computer file differently than a codex when it comes to ownership and usage rights. They are not the same in the eyes of the law nor for the companies selling them. That is a critical distinction and one we need to remain mindful of as we make decisions about our library collections during this tumultuous time of shifting format dominance. The debate over whether reading on the screen or the page is superior will continue for quite some time. The distraction of the Internet can detract from the reading experience (Bosman and Richtel 2012), and writers like Nicholas Carr have argued that our online life is damaging our ability to focus and take in long-form text. In response, many observers argue that the Internet is good for us, indeed that it may be expanding our definition of the mind (Zimmer 2009) and that all advances in technology have inspired some hand-wringing, from literacy itself to the printing press (Bell 2010).

It's tempting, especially for a librarian, to be too precious about books. Our profession is wrapped up in them, bound to them in many ways. However, our primary mission is to provide access to information, something that eBooks do quite well in some ways and horribly in others. Although ownership of a book is important to us institutionally, a library is not about individual ownership of books. We house our communities' collections, not our own and not those of individual members of the community. Still, we tend to understand books as objects and develop strong attachments to some of those objects.

The book lover's handwringing about the loss of the physical object could be short-sighted. James Bridle, of booktwo.org, argues that "while traditional books are physical objects, that's not the core of our relationship with them. The truth is that books are essentially not physical objects, but temporal ones" (Bridle 2010b). He goes on to explain that in one timeline of a reader's interactions with a book, the book starts as an advertisement (before it's been read), then is a vehicle for information delivery (while it's being read), and emerges as a souvenir. The eBook, he argues, delivers only on the middle part—the reading itself. The "social timeline of the book— the reviews you read before you buy it and the conversations you have with your friends about it and so on" (Bridle 2010a)—are not as clearly integrated into eBooks as they could be, nor are other aspects of book ownership, like appropriation, and books as souvenirs (a signed first edition, for example) (Bridle 2010a).

Bridle and others argue that what needs to be done is to "reactivate the book's temporal life, its aura, to create something we feel as passionate about as the physical book" (Bridle 2010b). (Bridle is using the word "aura" in a specific way here, citing Walter Benjamin's "The Work of Art in the Age of Mechanical Reproduction.") If the book's content is easily accessible, the connection that the reader feels to that book is the thing that becomes more valuable. The proliferation of sites and services (LibraryThing, Small Demons, Goodreads, etc.) designed to draw out the reader's experience with a text attests to the power of this idea.

Nate Hill, writing on the Public Library Association's blog, argues that those very sites and services are part of what make an eBook different from a book. The eBook version of a text inherently has potential that a paper copy doesn't. "The contents of that 'eBook' could be networked and intertwined with all other 'eBook' content across the web; contextual metadata about chunks of that 'eBook' content could be reused and repurposed to make other works . . . I'd suggest that because the properties of digital media mean this *can* happen then eventually it *will* happen. Everything eventually reaches it potential, in spite of artificial constraints" (Hill 2012).

What that realized potential will look like is still a matter of speculation. Our relationship with our books changes when we consume them as digital incarnations of themselves. Bridle spoke at the 2011 Books in Browsers conference, saying that we don't worry about Mp3 versus vinyl in the same way; we just say "music." We're hung up on the form with books, but Bridle suggests that there's a continuum, that digital is something "that acts on the continuum of the book rather than something that fundamentally changes it" ("Books in Browsers" 2011). Social sites like LibraryThing and Goodreads started their lives before eBooks had taken hold of a sizable chunk of the reading public, and Small Demons, which maps the songs, movies, books, people, foods, and other items mentioned in books and connects them to each other, was certainly possible without digital text. But the ability to easily parse and share the content of books changes how we interact with them, perhaps shifting our passion from the object to the story. Does that "reactivate the book's temporal life"? Or change how we see books altogether? Does it change again when we add games, interactive elements, and location awareness? Books have been with us for a long time, longer than any form of recorded music media. The person who collected records went on to collect CDs and now probably has terabytes worth of music stored on hard drives. Our collective and individual relationships with eBooks are just beginning. Whether we choose to see eBooks as something fundamentally different from print books or as something acting on the continuum of Book will impact the decisions we make both as readers and as stewards of library collections.

For now, though, we face a variety of issues and practicalities as we consider eBooks for our institutions. I don't think we can or should separate the philosophical from the practical, but I do think philosophical ambivalence can accompany practical decision making. The practicalities can quickly become overwhelming, not least because they change so quickly.

Keeping Up

It can feel nearly impossible to keep up with the onslaught of eBook information. There's no way to know everything that's happening with eBooks without devoting a sizable chunk of your workweek to the topic, but staying generally up-to-date is possible without neglecting your 9-5 duties. Sites you may already be visiting often cover eBooks, and many of them offer newsletters that come to your inbox daily or weekly.

Popular review site Shelf Awareness (http://www.shelf-awareness.com/) has a daily newsletter that covers the book industry.

Librarian favorite Early Word (http://www.earlyword.com/) links to major eBook news stories and has a weekly newsletter.

Romance review site Dear Author (http://dearauthor.com/) covers eBook stories and will send a daily digest to your inbox.

Library Journal's The Digital Shift (http://www.thedigitalshift.com/) posts daily on eBook issues and can be found on both Twitter and Facebook.

ALA's Digital Content and Libraries Working Group posts notes from their meetings and news updates on ALA Connect (http://connect.ala.org/node/159669) and they are releasing tip sheets on eBook topics (full disclosure: I am on one of the subcommittees and have worked on the tip sheets).

Outside of libraries, GalleyCat (http://www.mediabistro.com/galleycat/), Digital Book World (http://www.digitalbookworld.com/), and *Publishers Weekly* (http://www.publishersweekly.com) are all publishing-oriented sites that cover eBook news.

PaidContent (http://paidcontent.org/) and TeleRead (http://www.teleread.com/) both cover eBooks and update daily.

PBS's MediaShift (http://www.pbs.org/mediashift/) follows all things digital media related, including eBooks. They send out a weekly digest about a variety of topics of interest to libraries.

You don't have to follow all of these sites, or any of them. But if you're concerned about keeping up with eBooks, you might find that one or two of them give you the information you need without taking over your life. I'll also be posting updates to this book at http://www.ebookprimer.com

It's worth contemplating how we view, understand, and interact with print books and eBooks, not so much as a form of cultural and technological navel-gazing, but as a way of thinking about our own motivations and inclinations when we make practical decisions.

CHAPTER 2

The Rules of the Road

DIGITAL RIGHTS MANAGEMENT

DRM has gotten quite a bit of attention from librarians and consumers alike. There are groups devoted to ending DRM, including a group called Librarians Against DRM. DRM is any restriction that companies put on their eBooks to make sure that they can't be copied or easily passed around to other readers. Jason Griffey uses the analogy of DRM as a lock on an eBook, with the reader or app holding the key to that lock. Amazon, Griffey points out, could "remove all DRM from their files. This would mean that you'd still need a program to interpret the .amz, but you wouldn't need the key anymore" (Griffey 2010). Advocating for a lightweight DRM from the International Digital Publishing Forum (IDPF), Bill Rosenblatt defines DRM as "technology that encrypts content before distribution and requires users to employ special-purpose hardware or software to decrypt and view it" (Rosenblatt 2012).

Types of DRM

Amazon's Kindle, in addition to using its own format, also uses its own DRM. PDFs are often created without DRM, though Adobe's Adept DRM standard can be applied to a PDF, which means it can be read only in Adobe Digital Editions or on an eBook reader that supports Adept (such as a Nook or Sony Reader). ePub files work with three major varieties of DRM. Adobe's Adept standard, Barnes & Noble's Nook DRM (which works only on the Nook, though the Nook can also use Adobe's Adept), and Apple's Fairplay DRM.

What that means is that an ePub book encrypted with Apple's Fairplay DRM won't work on a Barnes & Noble Nook, even though the Nook can read ePub files. File type and DRM work in conjunction to control use of the file.

DRM was created by companies, but it's protected by Congress. The Digital Millennium Copyright Act, passed in 1998, makes it illegal to try to circumvent DRM (Lessig 2006, 117).

What's the Problem with DRM?

DRM often comes in the form of software designed to make digital files behave like nondigital objects—"an attempt to treat bits like atoms" (Worona 2007). Companies have used it in ways that range from seemingly reasonable to seemingly insane. DRM prevents more than one person from reading an eBook at once. This causes confusion for library patrons who don't understand why an eBook has a waiting list, but it makes a certain amount of intuitive sense—the library purchased one copy and it's being used one reader at a time. However, DRM also prevents purchasers of eBooks from loaning them, or prevents them from loaning an eBook more than once. This is where it starts to get strange. If DRM is designed to make an eBook behave like a paper book, limiting the number of times someone can loan a book they purchased doesn't make much sense to many readers. eBooks can be less flexible than print books when they're locked down by DRM.

DRM has been the source of some remarkably bad decisions made by companies in the past. Sony famously sold music CDs with DRM that allowed the company to access the purchaser's hard drive should they try to play it on their computer (Doctorow 2005). Companies have also used DRM to their ultimate disadvantage, creating products so difficult to use that customers give up trying. Library eBooks are potentially hampered by DRM this way. It is doubtlessly easier to pirate an eBook or simply buy it than it is to borrow it from the library.

For many publishers, DRM is seen as simply necessary. While there are companies publishing books without DRM, most see it as the only way to protect their content. Publishing industry consultant Mike Shatzkin cites Michael Tamblyn, CEO of Kobo, as saying that only 20 percent of books really need DRM, but it's a nonissue with consumers (Shatzkin 2011f). Most eReaders are single-person devices; a consumer buys a device, sets up an account with it, and simply buys eBooks. DRM becomes an issue when consumers want to switch to a different brand of device, or if they lose their purchases through hardware failure. Until that point, the eBook-buying public is likely to not give DRM a second thought. Many people may mistakenly assume they own the eBooks they buy, rather than license them. Author Cory Doctorow has been an outspoken opponent of DRM, especially in light of laws that make DRM even more powerful. Writing in the *Guardian*, Doctorow explained that DRM was bad for business: "If Tor [Doctorow's publisher] sells you one of my books for the Kindle locked with Amazon's DRM, neither I, nor Tor, can authorise you to remove that DRM. If Amazon demands a deeper discount (something Amazon has been doing with many publishers as their initial ebook distribution deals come up for renegotiation) and Tor wants to shift its preferred ebook retail to a competitor like Waterstone's, it will have to bank on its readers being willing to buy their books all over again" (Doctorow 2012c).

At Digital Book World 2012, Anobii CEO Matteo Berlucchi spoke about how to increase competition in the eBook market and took aim at DRM. He read a list called "If ebooks were paper books" that included items like, "If you need reading glasses, you can only read this book with glasses supplied by us," and "You can't give it to a friend" (Berlucchi 2012b). Although he listed DRM as "an important weapon to fight digital piracy," he cited the music industry's move away from DRM, beginning with record label EMI in 2007. Berlucchi characterized DRM as penalizing the good guys by treating them like bad buys and referred to a study done by researchers at Rice University and Duke University that found that DRM acts as an incentive to pirate content (Geere 2011). His suggestions for fighting piracy included taking infringers to court and educating the public. He emphasized using morality instead of DRM to encourage legal use of digital content. Using cloud management would ensure that access is controlled, and watermarks would play on people's morality and discourage piracy (who, after all, would put a file online illegally if it had their name and phone number in it?) (Berlucchi 2012b).

However, he also suggested that DRM would continue to be useful in a library setting. Drawing an analogy to the print world, he said library books are books we don't own, can't write in, and must return after a period of time has elapsed. DRM could be used to continue to make those things true of library eBooks. If the DRM were simple enough to navigate, that could work for libraries. It's true that right now loan periods are hard to achieve without DRM, though library values tend to support DRM-free books. Cory Doctorow's essay "Lockdown: The Coming War on General-Purpose Computing" tracks some of the early attempts to prevent software copying, none of which worked well, because technology caught up and changed, and making legal activity harder just makes illegal solutions easier. More regulation, Doctorow argues, does not stop illegal copying. "The important tests of whether or not a regulation is fit for a purpose are first whether it will work, and second whether or not it will, in the course of doing its work, *have effects on everything else*" (Doctorow 2012a). Doctorow uses wheels as an analogy, pointing out that even though wheels are crucial to the getaway cars used by bank robbers, lawmaking bodies wouldn't regulate the wheel. "We can all see that the general benefits of wheels are so profound that we'd be foolish to risk changing them in a foolish errand to stop bank robberies. Even if there were an epidemic of bank robberies—even if society were on the verge of collapse thanks to bank robberies—no-one would think that wheels were the right place to start solving our problems" (Doctorow 2012a).

Following that logic, DRM on purchased eBooks makes them less useful, but DRM on library eBooks could simply make them behave like library books. Ease of use is the paramount issue for libraries. If our eBooks are too difficult to use, they aren't useful to librarians or our patrons. An easy-to-use DRM that simply enforces loaning of library eBooks might be a compromise that libraries and publishers can live with. In May 2012, the International Digital Publishing Forum proposed a "lightweight DRM" for ePub books. Lightweight DRM would pose minimal intrusion to the end user, be simple to use, and be cheap to implement (Rosenblatt 2012). Clearly, this is not what we have in libraries currently.

DRM's days in the retail eBook marketplace may be numbered. In April 2012 TOR books, a division of Macmillian, announced they would be going DRM-free. Shortly after this announcement, Mike Shatzkin posted that he heard rumors at the London Book Fair that "two of the Big Six are considering going to DRM-free very soon. The rumor is from the UK side, but it is hard to see a global company doing this in a market silo" (Shatzkin 2012e). Shatzkin also commented on Pottermore's watermark success and recounted his conversation with Pottermore CEO Charlie Redmayne. Pottermore files are watermarked with the purchaser's name and other information and it's worth noting that although this has been hailed as "DRM-free," watermarking is seen by many as a form of lightweight DRM, though the IDPF's call for lightweight DRM specifically excludes watermarking from their definition of DRM (Rosenblatt, 2012). Redmayne

---

More on DRM

DRM is a hot topic all over the Internet. One of the most prolific writers on the topic is Cory Doctorow, who has a regular column in the *Guardian*—http://www.guardian.co.uk/profile/corydoctorow—in addition to his work at Boing Boing. He also has an eBook available for free that collects his essays about DRM. I can't recommend it enough if you're looking to get a deeper understanding of DRM and the issues surrounding it (see http://craphound.com/content/download/).

There are organizations (none of them in favor of DRM) that keep abreast of DRM-related news and issues:

Librarians Against DRM: http://readersbillofrights.info/
Defective by Design: http://www.defectivebydesign.org/
The Electronic Frontier Foundation's page on DRM: https://www.eff.org/issues/drm

told Shatzkin that after Pottermore files started appearing on file-sharing sites, other users chastised the people posting the eBooks: "C'mon now. Here we have a publisher doing what we've been asking for: delivering content DRM-free, across devices, at a reasonable price. And, by the way, don't you know your file up there on the sharing site is watermarked? They know who you are!" (Shatzkin 2012e). The content was removed by the posters before Pottermore could react. An anonymous publishing executive told PaidContent's Laura Hazard Owen that she or he now breaks DRM as a matter of course, not to share eBooks, but to own them (Owen, 2012c). These kind of high-profile experiments in selling eBooks without DRM (or with very lightweight DRM) may signal a major shift in the retail end of the eBook world. It remains to be seen what that will mean for libraries.

COPYRIGHT AND FIRST SALE

Intellectual property rights are enshrined in the U.S. Constitution. Article 1, Section 8 says that Congress has the power (among other things) "to promote the Progress of Science and useful Arts, by securing for limited Times to Authors and Inventors the exclusive Right to their respective Writings and Discoveries."

In 1790, Congress passed the first U.S. Copyright Act, which was modeled on the eighteenth-century English Statute of Anne. Authors were given a 14-year copyright, with one opportunity to renew for another 14 years ("A Brief History of Copyright and Innovation"). Over the course of the 1800s, a variety of types of artwork were added to the list of protected works. In 1901, the U.S. Copyright Act was revised to 28 years with an additional 28 on renewal. Copyright holders were required to register their copyright. In 1976, copyright was expanded to the life of the author plus 50 years after the author's death. This expansion applied only to works created in or after 1976. Exceptions to copyright like fair use were formalized, and the requirement that creators register their works was dropped ("Law and Technology Timeline").

Copyright has changed over time, as new technologies emerge and challenge the standards set by the law. Composers were given the right to profit off of recordings of their work (for a limited time) after the technology to create recordings posed a threat to their work. When broadcasting made it possible to share those recordings widely, Congress did not expand the law to include compensation for radio play (Lessig 2006, 172). Congress also decided not to criminalize use of cassette tapes. The Audio Home Recording Act allowed consumers to copy recordings onto tapes, either in their entirety or as part of mix tapes (Lessig 2006, 173).

Things got more complicated recently. In 1998, the Sonny Bono Copyright Term Extension Act added another 20 years, making the standard copyright the author's life plus 70 years. That year also saw the passage of the Digital Millennium Copyright Act, which provided exemptions for Internet service providers when their customers infringed upon copyright. Importantly, it also included "anticircumvention" rules, which apply when people try to break DRM ("Law and Technology Timeline").

Fair Use

Fair use is codified exceptions to copyright. For creators, this means that using someone else's work for things like parody, criticism and commentary, art, and scholarship are generally considered fair use (Fair Use Frequently Asked Questions). This doesn't mean that the creator won't get taken to court, just that they have a legal leg to stand on, though lawyers may have different perspectives when it comes to the legal use of fair use. Some are inclined to see it as a defense only, while others see it as "the space which the U.S. copyright system recognizes between the rights granted to copyright holders and the rights reserved to the public, where uses of works may or may not be subject to copyright protection" (Fair Use Frequently Asked Questions [and Answers]). Fair use is defined by factors that are defined in copyright law and each case is evaluated based on a subjective judgment of those factors. Stanford University Libraries' site on copyright and fair use gives this example: "one important factor is whether your use will deprive the copyright holder of income. Unfortunately, weighting the fair use factors is often quite subjective. For this reason, the fair use road map can be tricky to navigate" (Fair Use Stanford University Libraries).

For librarians and educators, teaching is another fair use exemption. This is why libraries have to secure licenses to show movies for entertainment, but classroom teachers do not when they show films for educational purposes. Libraries are also given special dispensation for interlibrary loan (Making Copies: Interlibrary Loan).

First Sale

The first-sale doctrine applies to physical objects. If you buy a book and then loan that book to a friend, you are not violating the author's copyright. If you buy a book and make a copy of it for a friend, you are. The first sale doctrine was codified in copyright law in Section 27 of the Copyright Act of 1909. By 1976, copyright law ensured that "copyright granted authors control over nothing by the work's initial publication" (Berube 2011). First sale requires ownership of a legal copy of the work. Libraries have been dependent on first sale; we need the right to loan purchased materials without having to get permission from the author or publisher each time a patron wants to borrow an item. Additionally, many libraries are heavily dependent on their patrons exercising their right to donate items under the first sale doctrine.

I am not a lawyer or a copyright expert, nor do I play either of those roles on television. Like most librarians, I know just enough to say "I think there might be a copyright issue here, let's find an expert," and I'm usually intimidated by copyright issues. I've found Nancy Sims's (aka the Copyright Librarian) blog very helpful: http://blog.lib.umn.edu/copyrightlibn/.

On Twitter, there's @LibraryLaw and @Copyrightlibn, both of whom tweet regularly about these (and other) issues.

ALA has a copyright page with useful resources: http://www.ala.org/advocacy/copyright.

The Electronic Frontier Foundation's Teaching Copyright page ("A Brief History of Copyright") is meant to help teachers incorporate copyright information into their lessons, but I found it very helpful in explaining the foundations of copyright: http://www.teachingcopyright.org/.

The University of Texas Libraries have a Copyright Crash Course ("Copyright in the Library") that is also extremely helpful: http://copyright.lib.utexas.edu/.

Stanford University Libraries has an excellent Copyright and Fair Use website, home to the Fairly Used blog: http://fairuse.stanford.edu/index.html

Section 117 of the US Copyright law outlines the conditions under which purchasers of software are allowed to make copies. For instance, creating an "archival" copy of a piece of software (otherwise known as backing up your hard drive) is allowed, but selling that archived copy is not (Copyright and Digital Files). Case law has generally placed responsibility for expanding first sale to digital objects with Congress and without intervention at the federal level, libraries are unlikely to gain first sale rights for eBooks (Berube 2011).

These principles have guided how libraries handle print materials. We can buy and loan books, we can buy and loan music, academic libraries can allow students and faculty to screen educational films, and we can copy journal articles for interlibrary loan (ILL). Once items are stored in a database, our relationship with them changes. Licensing agreements trump copyright law and the exceptions to that law that we have come to rely on.

LICENSING VERSUS OWNERSHIP

When you buy a book, you're buying a physical object, which, upon purchase, you own. The doctrine of first sale says that you can resell or loan that book, even if you want to loan it repeatedly, according to your own set of rules, as libraries do. The author's copyright extends to a digital version of that book, but the doctrine of first sale does not.

One of the biggest cultural changes of the past 20 years has been how we think about owning something. Our mental models for purchasing revolve around goods and services. We buy stuff or pay for people to do things for us. It's hard to get our minds around buying digital things. When the computer game/virtual world Second Life started making headlines, news stories regularly mentioned that while the game had its own currency, players had to spend real money to get Linden dollars. The thought of spending money on a digital environment bordered on the absurd, but "in-app" and other digital purchases are commonplace today.

Part of the difficulty of buying digital objects is that it once required some level of technical expertise. For someone who struggled to back up his or her own files, the idea of managing a library of Mp3s or early eBooks was overwhelming. As digital objects have become easier to own and more commonplace, the idea of spending money without getting a physical object in return has lost its initial strangeness. Anyone with a cable box can rent a movie, and while Starbucks still offers CDs as an impulse buy for the under-caffeinated, Mp3s are not a cutting-edge way to purchase music.

Similarly, as devices like Kindles and Nooks have dropped in price, eBooks have moved from the provenance of digital mavens and become a commonplace item. But ownership of an eBook remains confusing. For many people, the move to Mp3s began with ripping music off of CDs they already owned. When the iPod debuted, reviewers were given iPods loaded with music. They were also given the CDs, which Apple spent $50,000 on so as not to promote piracy (Fried 2001). Before cars came with CD players as a matter of course, it was perfectly acceptable to make yourself a copy of a CD on tape so you could play it in your car, as it is now considered acceptable to rip a CD to Mp3 for use on a digital music device ("Fair Use Frequently Asked Questions [and Answers]"). Personal mix tapes have also been widely seen as fair game, although in 2003, the Recording Industry Association of America's (RIAA) antipiracy spokesperson, Frank Creighton, told the *New York Times* that "while mixes on cassette tapes may not have inspired the wrath of the record industry in the past . . . digital mixes have better sound quality" (Gallagher 2003). Creighton cited the popularity of burning CDs for friends and relative and added that the RIAA would be foolish to publicly state that they would allow CD burning (Gallagher 2003). For the music industry, things got even messier when everything became a mix tape, when we started buying, trading, and taking music by the megabyte.

But not too many people are making their own eVersions of their personal libraries. Baby boomers (and their older offspring) aren't transitioning to Kindles by way of their scanners, the way they transitioned to iTunes by way of the "import CD" button (I'm singling out baby boomers and their kids as CD owners only because the so-called millennials have come of age with easy access to digital music and likely did not traipse off to college with CD towers as their older siblings did). Making the leap to owning music digitally, without a physical object, was shepherded by the actual process of digitizing music already owned in physical form.

With books, the process is often kick-started by the purchase of an eReader. Filling that eReader requires agreeing to a licensing agreement, but the notion of licensing a book is unfamiliar. We license software, sure, but that's something we use, a digital tool. A book isn't something we use to produce other things, but something we read. Ownership is part and parcel of our cultural understanding of books. The current eBook market requires us not only to purchase books that aren't objects but to purchase books we may not own.

The change in ownership models became very apparent in 2009 when Kindle owners who had purchased copies of Orwell's *Animal Farm* and *1984* found that those books had been removed and their cost refunded. The copies had been uploaded to the Kindle store illegally, and Amazon responded to the rights holder's complaint by removing the bootleg copies not only from the store but also from the devices of those who had already purchased it (Stone 2009). Amazon has since said they would not automatically remove purchased copies should this situation arise in the future (Pogue 2009). More recently, Maria Konnikova worried that booksellers were causing Jonah Lehrer's *Imagine* to vanish from existence after plagiarism accusations surfaced in 2012 (full disclosure: I cited an article by Lehrer in an earlier draft of this book, but removed it when I had a chance to make last-minute content changes in September 2012). She argues that "An e-book is not a physical book. That point might seem trite until you stop for a moment to think how much simpler it is, in a certain sense, to destroy electronic than physical traces" (Konnikova 2012). Although purchased Lehrer eBooks were not pulled from eReaders, Konnikova's concern highlights the difference between a discredited or out-of-date physical volume and, say, a website that's been taken down (Google cache and the Wayback Machine can only do so much).

The Orwellian Orwell incident reminded early Kindle owners exactly what the difference between licensing and ownership is. The conversation about the disappearing books on the Kindle discussion boards makes it clear that many Kindle owners were simply not aware that they did not own the content they purchased for their Kindles. Other anecdotal evidence suggests that ownership is still very much tied to the physical codex in most people's minds.

Carole Horne, the general manager of the Harvard Book Store, spoke to the *Boston Globe* about her customers buying multiple formats. She noted that they make a distinction between having a book on their iPad and owning it, that having something electronically doesn't feel like ownership to many of her customers (Katz 2011). This multiple-purchase system is certainly restricted to those with the disposable income to support an intensive book-buying habit. The impulse may even be restricted to book lovers who were already inclined to employ other multiple-purchase schemes, like buying a second copy of a book to lend to friends.

Ownership is of tremendous concern to librarians, since libraries have relied on the ability to own books in building their collections. Readers are less concerned about it. For publishers, ownership is a "horse out of the barn," according to publishing industry consultant Mike Shatzkin. Agreements that libraries are forging with smaller publishers to ensure ownership of eBooks are "distracting arguments on the fringes of commercial reality" (Shatzkin 2011f). The concern for publishers is that allowing ownership of a digital book will lead to a single sale of that book (Shatzkin 2011f), although we may still see a shift in reader attitudes about DRM. Lori James, COO and cofounder of All Romance eBooks, a site that sells (naturally) romance eBooks from a wide variety of publishers, reported at Digital Book World 2012 that books with DRM make up 91 percent of their inventory but only 4 percent of their sales and that 21 percent of their readers reported actively avoiding DRM because they wanted a book that was easier to use and they wanted to be able to do the things readers can do when they own a book, like share, print, read across multiple platforms, and so forth (James 2012).

While libraries might look for a DRM solution that treats library eBooks like print books, ownership of the materials by the library itself remains a concern. Libraries have typically defined themselves by their collections, though one could argue that it makes more sense to define the library by its services. A library's collection reflects the interests and character of its community, and the library's ability to buy, weed, and shape that collection to the changing needs and desires of its constituents has been central to the mission of the institution. As eBooks stand now, they are an additional service, an add-on, primarily for more affluent patrons, in the case of public libraries. An eBook collection cannot be added to in the same way a print collection can because not all publishers are willing to sell eBooks to libraries and they cannot be weeded or sold in book sales. More importantly, eBooks are available almost exclusively through vendors like Overdrive, 3M, and Baker and Taylor. As librarians have learned, painfully, through the transition to electronic journals, content that is available exclusively through vendors comes with many strings attached and never truly belongs to the library. Right now, eBooks are a special service, more an additional format than the bulk of a collection, but as eBook readership grows, the question of ownership will become increasingly important.

In 2012, Random House began offering eBook ownership but tripled the price of their eBooks. At the 2012 Massachusetts Library Association conference, Ruth Liebmann, director of account marketing at Random House, told the assembled librarians that they own their Random House eBooks (Maier 2012). In 2011, Random House allowed the Kansas State librarian to transfer the state library's Random House eBooks from Overdrive to 3M without repurchasing any titles (Kelley 2011e). Right now, that is the hallmark of eBook ownership, since other possibilities like ILL or reselling used eBooks aren't available for technical or legal reasons. The question libraries are pondering now is "Is that worth the cost increase?" For one Connecticut and one Canadian consortium, the answer is "no." Libraries Online Inc. (LION) and the South Shore Public Libraries in Nova Scotia both declared moratoriums on buying Random House's material (Kelley 2012a). In the case of LION, that extended to including exhorting members to boycott Random House's print materials as well (Libraries Online, Inc.). Access without ownership may very well be the preferred choice for libraries buying eBooks. A tiered model, with options to own and access on a per-title basis, is a popular concept, but it has yet to be offered by any publisher or vendor. The marketplace has not been producing solutions that are sustainable for libraries. As Andromeda Yelton asks, "If we buy into a status quo today that can triple ebook prices and slash how often a book can circulate overnight, what will be the terms for the must-have content of 2020? What content or services might we have to cut then to support the system we're cultivating now? When you have to choose whether the patron of 2012 and the patron of 2020 gets access to information, which do you choose, and why?" (Yelton 2012). Access is a key library value and right now, our hands are bound by the constraints of the marketplace, which has also complicated the issue of access. We first must determine if libraries have access to a title before we can consider our options for providing that title to our patrons. If the cost of ownership is too steep, we will be forced to make sacrifices in other areas (either now or in the future), limiting our patrons' access to other content. Bobbi Newman wondered on her blog if libraries should stop buying eBooks while still looking for better solutions saying, "I do not think we should stop looking for a solution or stop advocating on behalf of our patrons, but I do think perhaps we should stop throwing good money at a bad solution" (Newman 2012). So far, libraries

---

Points to Ponder

Products like O'Reilly's Safari Books Online and McGraw-Hill's eBook Library offer access to titles in rapidly changing subject areas, like technology and test prep. Depending on your community's interests, that model might be a good way to expand your library's offerings without investing heavily in an eBook platform.

Ownership may be assumed by your funding agencies. Make sure the folks signing the checks (and their lawyers) understand how your eBook arrangement works and that it may vary by publisher.

If ownership is important to you or your institution, but you want to offer eBooks, look for consortia in your area that allow nonmembers to join their eBook platform. It's even further away from ownership, but it can be a lower-cost way to offer eBooks with suboptimal licensing agreements.

have not found a workable place in the eBook ecosystem. Both ownership (such as it is) and licensing hamstring libraries in dramatic ways. Licensing versus ownership seemed like a fundamental issue just a year or two ago, but now seems like a false dichotomy that libraries must look beyond when contemplating their eBook futures.

CHAPTER 3

Market and Distribution Channels

CRUNCHING THE NUMBERS: EBOOK POPULARITY AND GROWTH

I'm guessing that you've picked up this book because you've been thinking a lot about eBooks. You might be finding the crush of information, opinion, and statistics overwhelming, the predictions depressing, and the way forward unclear. You might be excited for a tremendous digital future, and wondering when we're going to get there. Or neither of those things, or both of them at once. There are a lot of conflicting reports about the popularity of eBooks and eReaders. They're booming, but print still rules the day; and for many readers, they're a polarizing subject, with some committed to their eReaders and others declaring they will never buy eBooks ever. For many front-line librarians, it can feel like every other patron has an eBook question; and you may be seeing your print circulation dropping and wondering if an all-eBook future is imminent.

For now, let's look at where we are.

In September of 2011, Harris Interactive found that 15 percent of Americans owned an eReader ("One in Six Americans Now Use an E-reader"). Pew's Internet & American Life Project found that between mid-December 2011 and early January 2012, tablet ownership went from 10 percent to 19 percent and eReader ownership also jumped from 10 to 19 percent. Americans owning at least one tablet or eReader went from 18 percent to 29 percent. (Rainie 2012a) The percentages seem small, but considering that by some accounts fewer than half of all Americans purchase a book in a typical year, it's a sizable chunk of the book-buying public (Katz 2011). Pew's 2012 data found that

Readers of eBooks read more frequently than others

% of Americans age 16 and older who read every day or nearly every day
for these reasons

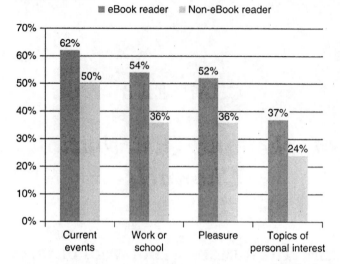

Data Source: Pew Research Center's Internet & American Life Reading
Habits Survey, November 16-December 21, 2011. N = 2,986 respondents
age 16 and older. Interviews were conducted in English and Spanish, and
on landlines and cells. The margin of error for the sample is +/–2 percentage
points. N for eBook readers = 739. N for non-eBook readers = 1,681.

22 percent of Americans have not read a book in the last 12 months (or refused
to answer the question), a number that has been steadily rising in Pew's research
since 1978, when 12 percent of those surveyed fell into those categories. By contrast, Pew found that the average eBook consumer has read 24 books in the last
year, compared with 15 books read by non-eBook readers. eBook readers also
report reading in all formats (Rainie 2012b).

The United States has seen a much higher rate of adoption of eReaders
than many other parts of the world. In the UK, just 3.7 percent of the population has either a tablet or an eReader. In Australia, only 0.9 percent.
Amazon, Barnes & Noble, and Apple are all U.S.-based companies, and
their products have been rolled out in the United States first. Other market
factors, like VAT (which in the UK applies to eBooks, but not printed
books), pricing strategy, and adoption of mobile technologies, also play a
role (Kearney and Bookrepublic 2011).

Online reading has been steadily rising. In April 2012, Pew released data
showing that one-fifth of Americans had read an eBook in the past year.
Their survey that ended in December 2011 used a broader definition of
eContent and found that 43 percent of Americans over the age of 16 had
read either an eBook or some other kind of long-form content on an eBook

Portrait of eBook readers – 29% of those who read books in the past
12 months

The % of the book readers 18+ in each group who read an eBook in the past 12 months.
* Asterisk denotes statistically significant difference with other rows.

	% of the book readers who read an ebook in the past 12 months
All those age 18 and older	29
Gender	
Male	29
Female	28
Age	
18–29	34*
30–49	34*
50–64	23
65+	17
Race and ethnicity	
White, non-Hispanic	29
Black, non-Hispanic	22
Hispanic (English- and Spanish-speaking	23
Educational attainment	
High school grad or less	19
Some college	34*
College graduate	35*
Household income	
Less than $30,000	20
$30,000–$49,999	25
$50,000–$74,999	35*
$75,000+	38*

Data Source: Pew Research Center's Internet & American Life Winter Tracking Survey, January 20-February 19, 2012. N = 2,253 adult respondents age 18 and older. Interviews were conducted in English and Spanish, and on landlines and cells. The margin of error for the sample is +/–2 percentage points. N for those who had read eBooks in the past 12 months is 321.

reader, a tablet, a computer, or a smartphone. Reading on one's phone always seems like a recipe for eye strain, but it's fairly common. Twenty-nine percent of those surveyed by Pew said they read eBooks on their phones (I recommend it as a way to avoid obsessive eMail checking when you're stuck in an airport or waiting room without a book). Not surprisingly, people in Pew's survey said they prefer eBooks for speed, selection, and reading while traveling or commuting, but print for sharing or reading with children (reading books in bed was a dead heat) (Rainie 2012b).

Pew also found that 19 percent of those in their libraries, patrons, and eBooks survey asked librarians or consulted library websites for book recommendations, while 14 percent of those who had read any books (print, eBook, or audiobook) in the last year got them from libraries. Pew's findings regarding eBooks and libraries will not surprise most librarians. Among those who do not read eBooks, 62 percent didn't know if their public library offered eBooks. Among eBook readers who do not get eBooks at their public library, 96 percent have not tried to download an eBook from the library. Those who had borrowed eBooks from their public library found the

Which is better for these purposes, a printed book or an eBook?

% of those who have read both eBooks and printed books in the last 12 months who say that this format is better for these purposes.

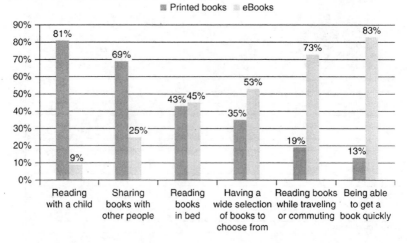

■ Printed books ■ eBooks

Data Source: Pew Research Center's Internet & American Life Reading Habits Survey, November 16-December 21, 2011. N = 2,986 respondents age 16 and older. Interviews were conducted in English and Spanish, and on landlines and cells. N for those who have read both printed books and eBooks in the past 12 months is 701.

selection surprisingly good. Thirty-two percent called the selection good; 34 percent called it excellent or very good. Twenty-three percent declared the selection fair, and 4 percent said it was poor, with 8 percent saying they didn't know. Paradoxically, of those who had borrowed eBooks from the library, 56 percent said they had found that the library did not carry an eBook they were looking for, and 52 percent said there was a waiting list to borrow a title they were looking for (Zickuhr 2012).

eReaders and tablets are very much on the rise, particularly as tablets become viable replacements for laptop computers. But what about eBook sales? eBook sales are steadily rising. In 2010, eBooks were 8.3 percent of revenue for larger publishing houses (or at least for the 15 that report data to the Association of American Publishers), and in 2011, that number was nearly 20 percent (Shatzkin 2011b). Research from R. R. Bowker found that eBook sales themselves (not the percentage of revenue) increased 17 percent in 2011. R. R. Bowker also found that 74 percent of book buyers have never purchased an eBook, but 14 percent of non-eBook buyers owned either a tablet or an eReader. Book sales generally are being driven by a relatively small group of power readers buying at least four books a month—a third of the buyers are responsible for two-thirds of growth (Dilworth 2012). Meanwhile, Verso Media found that among book buyers, the percentage of people who actively resist eBooks has gone up from 49 percent to 51 percent (Verso Digital 2011). "This data point is in line with other tea

How readers got the most recent book they read
% of those who read a book in the last 12 months who got the book by...

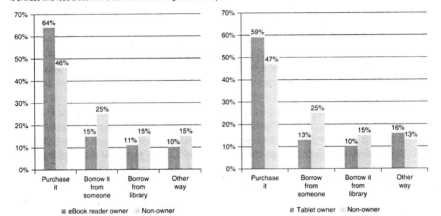

Data Source: Pew Research Center's Internet & American Life Reading Habits Survey, November 16-December 21, 2011. N for the number of those who had read a book in the past 12 months = 2,474 among those age 16 and older. Interviews were conducted in English and Spanish, and on landlines and cells. The margin of error for the sample is +/–2 percentage points. N for eBook reader owners = 676. N for tablet owners = 638.

leaves that suggest that we might have started to hit real resistance to ebooks, slowing down the digital switchover from the rates of the past few years" (Shatzkin 2012d).

The Verso Media study is worth paying attention to. They found that avid book buyers, which they defined as people who buy 10 or more books a year, are 20 percent of the U.S. population over 18 (they also found that 22 percent of the population doesn't buy books at all). Their study also concluded that eReader sales have moved out of the early-adopter phase, with 16 percent of those surveyed (the survey was conducted between November 30, 2011, and December 4, 2011) saying they already had eReaders (22% of avid readers surveyed already have eReaders) and 16 percent saying it was very or somewhat likely they would be purchasing one in the next year. However, they also found that resistance to eReaders is on the rise from 40 percent in 2009 to almost 52 percent in 2011. Tablet ownership, meanwhile, has lower resistance (46%) and higher planned purchasing (21% say they are somewhat or very likely to buy a tablet in the next year). Both eReader and tablet owners planned to purchase equal numbers of eBooks and print books (Verso Digital 2011). Verso's findings are similar to *Library Journal*'s Patron Profiles study, which found that library "Power Patrons," who visit the library weekly, are also regular buyers of books. In fact, *Library Journal* found that all library patrons purchase, on average, 11 books a year, making them "avid" patrons by Verso's reckoning. eBook readers, though a smaller segment of *Library Journal*'s sample, were active buyers of print and eBooks, as well as regular library users (Verso Digital, 2011 and Phaxia 2011).

National statistics are fantastic, though the number of news stories touting the latest figures can be overwhelming. As I've said before, I rely on Pew's research in this area. I think it helps to have national figures in mind when we think about eBooks. I always encourage librarians to try to gauge what's going on in their own communities with eBooks, but it's easy to be swayed by a few anti-eBook patrons or the handful of regulars who haven't come in as often since they got a Kindle. It's good to have local stories in your back pocket for funding challenges, and it's also helpful to be able to cite Pew's research showing that eReader owners still read print as well. Libraries are still seen predominantly as book places, and we are, but if you're considering piloting a project to loan objects like tools, cake pans, or musical instruments, do it! Other library services and programs can serve as vivid reminders to funding agencies that the library won't be felled by eBooks.

Many of these findings are in line with library anecdotes. Librarians have told me that some of their regular, active patrons have purchased eReaders and begun to visit the library less often. People who buy eReaders are often the most voracious readers—why else buy a device dedicated to reading? For publishers, the percentage of revenue coming from digital books seemed to be growing exponentially, but that growth may slow if eReader resistance remains high. Verso predicts that 25 to 30 percent will have an eReader or tablet within the next few years, but 50 percent will remain resistant (Verso Digital 2011). Humans are notoriously bad at predicting their own behavior, so it will be interesting to see these studies repeated over the next three to five years.

MARKET OVERVIEW: EREADER AND EBOOK VENDORS

There are a tremendous number of eBook vendors out there. Small publishers often sell eBooks directly to customers, and independent bookstores can sell eBooks on their websites. There are even a few online-only bookstores, like Emily Books (a bookstore that has actively chosen to sell books without DRM). Authors who self-publish online through Amazon and Barnes & Noble can sell their books through affiliate links on their websites. There's no shortage of places to buy eBooks.

I'm focusing on the major consumer players here: Amazon, Barnes & Noble, and Apple. Not coincidentally, all three also sell devices. The consumer eBook market is bigger and more interesting than just those three vendors, but they are the proverbial 800-pound gorillas. Amazon dominates the market in part because the Kindle came out well before the Nook or the iPad, and in part because they sell both device and content. Kindle is the top-selling eBook device, though Amazon does not release exact figures. In addition to being the only vendor of the most popular device, Amazon is now a publisher as well.

For consumers, Amazon has been portraying itself as the upstart rabble-rouser, unseating the big publishing houses from power (Streitfield 2011). For many would-be authors, this rings true—Amazon has given them an opportunity to get their work read. For publishers (and to some extent, libraries), Amazon is a Goliath, using its retail and eBook dominance to dictate how publishers do business. The eBook market looks very different to each of the players.

When it comes to libraries, there are any number of vendors, and different companies jump in and out of the library eBook scene. Whatever is true now will certainly have changed by the time this book is published and changed again by the time you're reading this. Some companies specialize in academic library needs (like EBL), while others (like OverDrive) serve mostly public libraries.

I'm giving only brief overviews of each of these companies. The products each company offers are likely to change before this book is published, and there will doubtless be product announcements aplenty at ALA's annual conference in 2012. At the beginning of 2012, rumors began spreading that Barnes & Noble might spin its Nook business off into a separate company, followed by a partnership with Microsoft to form a new company with Barnes & Noble's eBook and educational sales. Apple may release a smaller iPad, which could encroach on Kindle Fire and Nook tablet sales. Librarians are good at research, and if you're looking to buy a device or your library wants to compare eBook vendors, a book isn't going to be much help, anyway. I've tried, instead, to include a general sense of the types of products each company offers, with a little bit of speculation about where each is headed in the future.

APPLE

With the release of the iPad, Apple jumped into the eBook market with iBooks and the iBookstore. Books purchased from the iBookstore can be read on iOS devices (iPads, iPhones, and iPod Touches) but not on Mac OS or any other PC operating systems.

Apple does not have a mechanism that allows for libraries to use the iBookstore at this time. So why should libraries care about their eBooks? As of August 2011, Apple's mobile operating system, iOS, accounted for 43.1 percent of mobile web traffic in the United States, with iPads counting for 97 percent of tablet traffic (ComScore 2011). A lot of people are using iPhones and iPads. Apple devices do have apps for other eBook vendors, including Amazon, Barnes & Noble, and OverDrive, but those apps manage the user's eBooks from other vendors—it does not connect the iBookstore content with OverDrive.

Apple paved the way for publishers to sell eBooks using the agency-pricing model, where the publishers set the price of the book and give the vendor a percentage of what they sell (Levine 2011, 159). For Apple, this mirrors their app store structure—Apple takes a 30 percent commission on sales of apps and treats books sold in the iBookstore much the same way. Book-app hybrids are also growing in popularity in the app store. For example, Loud Crow Interactive is working with Peanuts Worldwide to create a series of "interactive digital book apps" based on Peanuts television shows, beginning with "A Charlie Brown Christmas" ("Peanuts and Loud Crow Partner"). While the Peanuts apps will be available for a variety of platforms, some attention-grabbing apps like Faber's app of T. S. Eliot's poem "The Waste Land," and *The Fantastic Flying Books of Mr. Morris Lessmore* (Shankland 2011) are exclusive to the iPad ("The Waste Land for iPad").

In January 2012, Apple announced an update to the iBookstore and new products designed for the education market. Apple's digital textbooks will be sold through iBooks 2 and will be initially targeted at the K–12 market. The play for the textbook market has been seen as part of Steve Jobs's vision for the company. Commenting on the company's product launch, ReadWriteWeb's John Paul Titlow said, "In his official biography of Apple's late cofounder, Walter Isaacson revealed that in addition to television and photography, one industry Steve Jobs was hoping to revolutionize next was textbooks, which he saw as being 'ripe for digital destruction.' Today's demonstration very much echoed Jobs' vision for textbooks, which he saw as cumbersome, heavy and slow to update. By contrast, the iPad is portable, interactive and of course quite easy to update with new information" (Titlow 2012).

Apple also revealed iBooks Author, an app for creation of textbooks. Though the initial response to both iBooks 2 and iBooks Author was largely positive, the enthusiasm that followed the demonstration was damped by the end user license agreement (EULA) that accompanied iBooks Author. The *Guardian*'s higher education blog reported that "the reaction from both the technology and the education communities was swift and emphatic" (Anyangwe 2012), pointing to Mashable editor Lance Ulanoff's post. Ulanoff enthuses that, with the right hardware, Apple could usher in "the dawn of a new age in education" (Ulanoff 2012). As more people became familiar with the EULA, though, criticism mounted.

Specifically, when a would-be author exports a book from iBooks Author, a window pops up saying that you are about to "create a version of your book that can be read using iBooks on your iPad." The would-be author is also warned that "books can only be sold through the iBookstore."

In the license agreement, the second paragraph states:

IMPORTANT NOTE:
If you charge a fee for any book or other work you generate using this software (a "Work"), you may only sell or distribute such Work through Apple (e.g., through the iBookstore) and such distribution will be subject to a separate agreement with Apple.

Many commentators have taken issue with this requirement, while others have defended it. On the Cult of Mac, Mike Elgan wrote that the terms are optional because, "Apple's iBooks Author is just an offer. . . . Nobody is being coerced. On the contrary, Apple's terms aggressively champion the cause of free books. There are several powerful incentives for authors to give books away free. Who wrote this policy, [Free Software advocate and founder of GNU Project] Richard Stallman? Apple's authoring tool is free, and if you don't charge for the book, you can distribute it anyway you like" (Elgan 2012). While using iBooks Author certainly is optional, blogger and iOS developer Dan Wineman points out that the license agreement "attempts to restrict what I can do with the *output* of the app, rather than with the app itself. No consumer EULA I've ever seen goes this far. Would you be happy if Garage Band required you to sell your music through the iTunes Store, or if iPhoto had license terms that kept you from posting your own photos online? It's a step backward for computing freedom and we should resist it" (Wineman 2012).

Apple's products have traditionally been aesthetically pleasing, user-friendly, and innovative. However, they are not open source, though usually not any more so than other proprietary vendors. Apple has a history with the education market, and if their textbook platform takes off, it will be interesting to see if they extend the restrictiveness of this license agreement to other areas of the Apple universe.

BARNES & NOBLE

Barnes & Noble released the Nook (now called the Nook First Edition) in 2009, after just six months of development (Bosman 2012b). Since its original release, Barnes & Noble has offered the Nook Color (2010), the Nook Simple Touch (2011), the Nook Tablet (2011), and the Nook Simple Touch with Glow Light (2012). All Nooks allow most library eBooks to be loaded onto the devices, using Adobe Digital Editions to manage the transfer and the library loan periods. Nooks also feature a lending ability for purchased books, though this is restricted to a single loan of loanable books for a 14-day period.

Barnes & Noble sells eBooks that can be read on their readers and apps only, using the ePub format. Because the Nook has been OverDrive-friendly since its inception, public libraries have had success in working with local Barnes & Noble outlets to promote library eBooks to customers buying Nooks. The company is in the unenviable position of being the last major bookstore chain standing (although Books-A-Million took over the leases of 14 Borders outlets) with many watching it as a bellwether of the book market.

The company is struggling; as the *New York Times* reported, "No one expects Barnes & Noble to disappear overnight. The worry is that it might slowly wither as more readers embrace e-books" (Bosman 2012b).

Barnes & Noble represents a tremendous amount of shelf space for publishers, but, "what if all those store shelves vanished, and Barnes & Noble became little more than a cafe and a digital connection point? Such fears came to the fore in early January, when the company projected that it would lose even more money this year than Wall Street had expected. Its share price promptly tumbled 17 percent that day" (Bosman 2012b).

Although independent booksellers are enjoying a renaissance in the wake of Borders' closing, "in many locales, Barnes & Noble is the only retailer offering a wide selection of books. If something were to happen to Barnes & Noble, if it were merely to scale back its ambitions, Amazon could become even more powerful and—well, the very thought makes publishers queasy" (Bosman 2012b). Barnes & Noble did announce in early January 2012 that it was considering spinning off the Nook business. *Fortune* magazine contributor Dan Mitchell endorsed the idea, saying that "the company is admitting that it can't finance the future of the book business while it's still lashed to the past of the book business. Or, more precisely, it *could* finance the future of the book business if only investors would look the other way for a few years and let the company lose lots of money while it did so. But of course investors won't do that" (Mitchell 2012). Nook sales have exceeded expectations, but haven't been enough to keep company earnings up. As of January 2012, Nook has 27 percent of the eBook market (Bosman 2012b).

In April 2012, Barnes & Noble announced that they would spin off their Nook business along with their college division into a new subsidiary. The new company will be partially owned by Microsoft, which invested $300 million for its 17.6 percent stake. Analysts generally saw this as a good move for both companies when it was announced (Ovide 2012).

AMAZON

Amazon released the Kindle in 2007, marking a turning point in the adoption of eBooks. Libraries responded by buying the devices to loan to patrons, prompting a tremendous amount of discussion on the legality of loaning eBooks by loaning devices. However, Kindle owners could not use library eBook offerings on their devices, which became increasingly problematic as the Kindle grew in popularity. Since the initial release of the Kindle, Amazon has updated the device several times. As of this writing, the fifth iteration of the Kindle is available, along with the Kindle Paperwhite, the Kindle Keyboard, and the Kindle Fire line, which includes an HD version of the tablet as well as an HD tablet with a larger screen. Amazon added the ability to loan Kindle books to other Kindle users in 2010 and began offering Kindle library eBooks via OverDrive in September of 2011.

Kindle owners can select titles through OverDrive's interface and click on the link to borrow the Kindle version. The loan is handled through Amazon's website, and content is delivered via Wi-Fi, but not 3G. For

Kindles that have only 3G, the eBooks must be transferred to the device from the owner's computer. The checkout process has been praised as relatively easy by librarians, and called "clunky but awesome" by at least one technology blogger (Anderson 2011).

The lack of Kindle compatibility for library eBook vendors was a sore spot for many librarians. Public librarians faced scores of Kindle-toting patrons who were, at best, heartbroken and, at worst, vitriolic that the library could not offer eBooks for the Kindle. The rollout of Kindle library books (which was begun without offering libraries advanced notification of exact dates, anecdotally causing confusion for front-line library staff caught unaware) highlights some of the larger issues surrounding eBooks in libraries. Concerns about the library's role in the relationship between Over-Drive, Amazon, and patrons as well as threats to patron privacy were brought to the fore by the Amazon-centered loaning mechanism, and the company's retention of patrons' notes and highlighting. Notices that a book's lending period has elapsed come from Amazon and prominently offer the option to buy the book, raising the hackles of many librarians (Houghton 2011a) and even some patrons (West 2011a), some more so than others (Schneider 2011). Others note that Kindle owners have already agreed to Amazon's terms and conditions and were happy giving their personal information to Amazon. As Karen Schneider points out, "That conversation changes with the first person (or library) who purchases a Kindle in order to check out "free" (to them) library books" (Schneider 2011).

Amazon has also begun their own lending program for Amazon Prime customers. For $89 a year, the Prime member gets free two-day shipping on Amazon-sold items, access to a larger collection of free streaming video online, and if the Prime customer is also a Kindle owner (apps are not included), access to one free book a month, from a selection of titles. The number of titles offered in Amazon's lending library has grown continuously since the product's beginning (Kelley 2011b). By January 2012, Amazon reported there were over 75,000 books in the lending library and by September 2012, Amazon's website offers 145,000 titles in the lending library. Large publishers have been reluctant to join Amazon's lending program, so they launched KDP Select, which is a fund designed to attract independent authors to the program. For a KDP author or publisher that makes a book available exclusively on Amazon for at least ninety days, the book can be included in the lending library and earn the author money from the KDP fund (Rao 2012). Speaking at Digital Book World 2012, Amazon's vice president for Kindle content, Russ Grandinetti, said that while publishers give books away in a "coarse effort to stimulate demand," the Kindle lending program is a targeted promotion to core (Prime) customers and publishers and authors get paid for the loan. He went on to say that borrowing drives word of mouth, reviews, and recommendations and cited *The Hunger Games* as an example. Kindle owners who borrowed *The Hunger Games* went on to buy the next two books in the series, rather than wait to borrow them in subsequent months (Grandinetti 2012) (though *Hunger Games* may not be the best example as it is the first in a wildly popular series).

As Amazon develops as a publisher (they've already signed Tim Ferris, James Franco, and Penny Marshall to their imprint), they'll continue to affect the market enormously. They have the dominant eReader, they sell more print and eBooks than anyone, and they have the money to back their riskier ventures. Right now, the market is theirs to lose.

LIBRARY VENDORS: OVERDRIVE

OverDrive is, as of this writing, the top dog in the library eBook marketplace, at least as far as public libraries are concerned. According to their website, they count 15,000 libraries worldwide as customers, 11,000 of them in the United States. The size of their customer base has given the company leverage, allowing them to negotiate the integration of Kindle-compatible eBooks for library users.

The company's web platform has patron and staff interfaces, but patrons can also borrow eBooks via OverDrive's Media Console, an application that runs on both desktops and mobile devices. OverDrive's latest product, announced in 2011, is WIN (which stands for Want It Now), an opt-in feature that allows patrons to buy titles through OverDrive, with the library earning affiliate fees on sales. The WIN catalog will include both eBooks that the library offers and content from publishers that do not offer library lending ("Entire eBook Catalogs to be Available").

OverDrive dominates the library market but is being challenged by newer entrants into the public library eBook market. In recent months, OverDrive has been caught in the middle between publishers changing their policies for library lending and librarians frustrated by those changes. Librarians have wondered on list servs and among themselves if other vendors will be able to strike different deals with publishers, but as of yet there is little evidence that that will be the case so far. The state librarian of Kansas has gained national attention for her move from OverDrive to 3M. Joanne Budler ended the Kansas Digital Library Consortium's contract with OverDrive when the new contract included a 700 percent increase in cost and changed the wording of the contract to exclude ownership of the content purchased through OverDrive (Landgraf 2012). Budler consulted Kansas deputy attorney general Jeffery Chanay, who agreed that the consortium's 2005 contract allowed for ownership while the new one did not. The consortium (and the attorney general's office) contacted publishers and was able to move 73 percent of the eBook content to 3M's platform and 63 percent of their audiobooks to Recorded Books: OneClickdigital ("Newsmaker: Joanne Budler" 2012).

Steve Potash, the CEO and founder of OverDrive, spoke at Digital Book World 2012, saying that he went to his first ALA in 2002 and started asking librarians "how do you want it to work?"—a question he continues to ask of his customers. He hinted at the company's future plans, saying that Amazon has all the data and DRM wasn't invented to frustrate library patrons. Potash said that OverDrive will give librarians access to their data, but added that he's fed up with anecdotal stories and wants to aggregate data for authors and publishers to show how library patrons discover new eBooks. "Discovery" is a publishing watchword when it comes to eBooks, and offering that data to publishers could be a powerful negotiating tool for OverDrive. It could also help prove the library's role in the eBook marketplace. OverDrive has been working with public libraries longer than any other eBook vendor, and that wealth of data could be key to maintaining their position of dominance in the library eBook market.

LIBRARY VENDORS: 3M

3M is the new kid in the library eBook market. Historically, the company sold security for collections, RFID, and self-check to libraries. Their Cloud Library product marks a foray into content. Tellingly, the breadcrumbs on 3M's Cloud Library page put library products under "Safety, Security, and Protection," which is a more typical description of the products that 3M sells to libraries. However, the company hired Library Journal book review editor Heather McCormack in August 2012 to lead their collection development efforts ("LJ Book Review Editor Heather McCormack to Manage 3M Ebook Lending Collection Development" 2012), a move which will no doubt bring the company up to speed very quickly on library content. 3M launched the product at ALA's annual conference in 2011, partnering with the German company txtr to create the platform. In addition to the Cloud Library itself, 3M also offers their own readers for libraries to loan to patrons and discovery terminals where patrons can look for and borrow content. Because the system is account based, patrons can borrow a book from a terminal, or a PC, and read it on a handheld device. As of this writing, 3M has a group of beta testers who went live on the system in the spring of 2012 (Bane 2012), and began rolling the service out in April of 2012 (the Kansas State Library keeps a beta progress page on their website, detailing their 3M launch: http://www.kslib.info/kansas-ez-library/beta-progress-3m.html). A larger group of early adopters will start using the Cloud Library after that. Beta testers and early adopters were required to purchase discovery terminals and eReaders as part of their partnership with 3M (Bane 2012). The service was made available for purchase at ALA Annual 2012.

3M's interface is relatively easy to use and allows patrons to create a username and password to sign in across multiple platforms, which is more user-friendly than requiring a library card number for each checkout. The company has gotten a lot of attention for their easier checkout process.

It remains to be seen if libraries will use 3M and OverDrive simultaneously, or move to 3M entirely. Ownership of OverDrive collections will likely be a deciding factor. If libraries and consortia can follow the route that Kansas did (Kelley 2011e), they may be more inclined to migrate their collections.

LIBRARY VENDORS: BAKER AND TAYLOR

Baker and Taylor has been working with K-NFB's Blio reader. K-NFB is a joint venture between Kurtzweil Technologies and the National Federation of the Blind (NFB), and they released their Blio reader in September 2010. Baker and Taylor worked with publishers to make content available for Blio. Blio was available to consumers for about a year before Baker and Taylor brought it to the library market. It comes preinstalled on a number of brands of PC and is free to download.

Accessibility is key among Blio's features, thanks to its origins with the NFB. A January 2012 article from *Braille Monitor* criticized Blio's accessibility, saying details had been "overlooked or poorly implemented" (Mason 2012). Baker and Taylor representatives have said that these issues are being resolved. Given the product's association with the NFB, accessibility will likely be a high priority as Blio is improved. For libraries, Baker and Taylor is offering a digital media platform called Axis 360. Not all titles on Axis 360 are available for use with Blio. Baker and Taylor's eBooks did not initially come in the ePub format, though ePub compatibility was planned. Integration with print purchases through TitleSource is one of their main selling points, along with the low cost of the eReading platform. Baker and Taylor actively pursued smaller libraries, "because the company noticed many of them were relying on consortial arrangements to afford startup costs of ebook platforms but that, once in the consortium, they sometimes felt they were not getting equal access to content" (Kelley 2012e). The company is also adding content from the self-publishing site Smashwords to Axis 360.

Baker and Taylor has a long history with libraries and other library vendors. Although Axis 360 currently does not have the same depth of content or device compatibility that other eBook vendors offer, those features are more easily developed than the long-term relationships that Baker and Taylor already enjoys. However, the eBook market has often proved indifferent to the partnerships of the past.

LIBRARY VENDORS: FREADING

Freading is a service of Library Ideas LLC, the same company that offers Freegal, a music service for libraries, and Rocket Languages, an online language-learning platform for libraries. Freading is structured differently from other public library-oriented eBook services. There is no annual platform fee, and libraries pay by circulation. Freading also offers simultaneous use, though libraries pay for each use individually ("Freading").

eBooks from Freading can be read on a computer, a Nook, an iPad or iPhone, most Android tablets and phones, the Kobo eReader and Vox tablet, and, with a few extra steps to install the app, the Kindle Fire. As with Over-Drive, Freading requires the user to sign up for an Adobe Digital Editions account. Freading uses a token system to loan books to patrons. Books are assigned a token value—four, two, or one tokens, with newer books usually starting at four tokens and dropping over time. Patrons are given a certain number of tokens a week by their libraries, which they can see when they log into their Freading accounts. They can roll tokens over week to week for a four-week period, after which all unused tokens disappear and the patron is back to their one-week allotment. Freading does not share the list of publishers available through the platform ("FAQ" Freading). Freading is a newcomer to the library eBook market and their product operates very differently from most of the other vendors. The token system is a bit complicated, particularly if Freading is being offered in conjunction with another eBook service. Librarians I've spoken to about the service have been enthusiastic about simultaneous access and the ease of operation for library staff—there's no selection process or book buying that has to take place. The trade-off is in complexity for patrons and possibly less selection of materials (we can't compare, since Freading doesn't release its publisher list).

LIBRARY VENDORS: INGRAM

Ingram's eBook product is called MyiLibrary, an online eBook interface. eBooks can be transferred to an eReader using Adobe Digital Editions, but they can also be browsed or read on the screen ("MyiLibrary demo"). Because access is offered primarily through a website, simultaneous use (of up to three users) is possible. The publishers available to MyiLibrary customers are largely academic (Random House and Penguin were not among them in late 2011, prior to Penguin's announcement that they would not offer new eBooks to public libraries), though Ingram's website advertises popular nonfiction subject areas (Test Prep, Resumes) to potential public library purchasers. The web interface is designed for researchers and students to search a book for keywords and print or (if the publisher allows it) download a selection of pages ("MyiLibrary demo"). In April 2011, Ingram announced a partnership with OCLC to loan MyiLibrary content via OCLC's WorldCat Resource Sharing. Under this program, a nine-day loan costs the library 15 percent of the cost of the eBook. When the program was announced, only half of the titles in MyiLibrary were available to loan, but Ingram expected the number to rise as more publishers agreed to the arrangement (Rapp 2011b).

Ingram also announced in April 2011 that it would be moving all of its digital audiobook customers off of MyiLibrary and onto Recorded Books OneClickdigital platform. Both Ingram and Recorded Books continue to sell eAudiobooks, which can be used with the OneClickdigital interface. Rich Rosy, VP and general manager of Ingram Library Services, told *Library Journal* that the arrangement allowed Ingram to effectively double their eAudiobook offerings by allowing Ingram to sell Recorded Books content (Rapp 2011b).

Ingram has been a major public library vendor on the print side, so it's a bit surprising that they haven't expanded their eBook offerings to include major publishers and fiction. Right now, vendors are specializing by market, with very little crossover. Although Ingram is marketing some of their titles to public libraries, it would be a supplemental collection at best, and for many libraries, a second eBook vendor simply means another place for patrons to search, another interface for everyone to learn, and another platform fee to budget for. Companies that have a history of working with libraries might have a minor sales advantage, but without the content, they'll always be a tertiary player.

LIBRARY VENDORS: NETLIBRARY/EBSCO

"What's the story with NetLibrary?" is a question that passes the lips of public librarians from time to time. NetLibrary was founded in 1998, filed for bankruptcy in 2001, and was purchased by OCLC in January of 2002 (Jackson 2004). As a subsidiary of OCLC, NetLibrary partnered with Gale, EBSCO, and Elsevier to offer content (Jackson 2004). By 2004, NetLibrary was offering content from Recorded Books, making it appealing to public libraries. The year 2007 brought lawsuits, with NetLibrary and Recorded Books suing each other for breach of contract, violation of copyright, unfair competition, and defamation (Pinkowski 2007). OCLC sold NetLibrary to EBSCO in 2010 (Oder 2010) and a year later debuted a platform that integrated NetLibrary content with EBSCO's database content (Kelley 2011c).

EBSCO's eBooks come in two packages. There are EBSCO eBooks, which are limited to a small selection of large academic publishers and can be purchased individually or in subject-specific collections. There are also EBSCO eBooks on EBSCOhost, which offers a wider array of titles, including a general reference package and a children and young adult collection. Again, EBSCO is promoting its custom collections and subject sets built by EBSCO staff. Their primary acquisitions model is ownership, though their website promises that lease and subscription options are forthcoming. They do offer multiple access models for their titles, and eBooks can be downloaded to a variety of devices (including the Nook and Sony eReader). The titles appear to be mostly academic and school library oriented, with public library packages that emphasize reference works and the homework needs of schoolchildren and teens. EBSCO also offers corporate, government, and medical collections for special libraries.

LIBRARY VENDORS: EBRARY

ebrary was founded in 1999 by two friends who wanted to help libraries acquire and offer information digitally. The company was purchased by ProQuest in 2011 ("Company" ebrary). Their content focus is nonfiction, with subject bundles and individual titles available for libraries. They feature patron-driven acquisitions and short-term loans prominently, and many of their titles offer pricing for either single- or multiple-use titles ("Prepackaged Products"). ebrary has a strong history of innovation. In 2011, Eric Hellman profiled the company, saying "ebrary has also been an innovator in business models as well as in technology. ebrary's initial model was to make ebooks available for free viewing; rights-holders were compensated using a micro-transaction model where subscribers were charged every time they did things such as print pages. Based on customer feedback, they shifted to a model where most content is available for use with on flat subscription fee" (Hellman 2011c). In 2012, ebrary released apps for iPhones and iPads. Although the company's focus is on academic libraries, they do offer public library packages. The company's Public Library Complete offers 28,000 titles with simultaneous access. The content is largely reference material, but includes about 500 Spanish-language titles. Public libraries that subscribe to the collection generally say they are looking for a complement to their OverDrive subscription (Kelley 2012b).

LIBRARY VENDORS: EBL

EBL, or eBook library, explicitly focuses on academic and research libraries. They tout their concurrent lending, which they call "Non-Linear Lending," as well as other academically oriented features like short-term loans and chapter reserves ("About eBook Library"). The company is part of Ebooks Corporation, an Australian company, which also owns ebooks.com, a digital bookstore. EBL works with an advisory board of academic libraries to develop its model for eBook sales to libraries. Their entire list of publishing partners is available on their website. In keeping with their customer base, the publishers are predominantly academic and technical ("About eBook Library").

In *The No Shelf Required Guide to E-Book Purchasing*, Susan Hinken and Emily J. McElroy detailed the Orbis Cascade Alliance's move to consortial purchasing of ebooks. Both EBL and ebrary were well liked by members of the 36-library alliance, with EBL's pricing model gaining high marks. Of the various pricing and purchasing models offered, the consortium gave a subscription model the highest score, with pay-per-view, demand-driven, and hybrid models falling slightly behind. Collection-based purchases were the least favorite for the librarians (Hinken and McElroy 2011, 11).

LIBRARY VENDORS: FOLLETT

Follett works entirely with the school library market. They offer an ILS, print book purchasing, and eBooks to school media specialists. Their integration of purchasing, cataloging, OPAC, and downloading is one of their primary selling points. Even their website is incredibly teacher-friendly, offering alternative links to TeacherTube for their videos in case YouTube is blocked by school administrators and IT. Follett offers eBook bundles in subject- and curriculum-oriented packages for K–12 schools. Many of their titles have the option of unlimited simultaneous access within a school building. The company offers an access platform called FollettShelf that can be used in conjunction with an existing OPAC to offer eBooks ("eBook FAQs"). They have also developed iPad applications for their eBook customers.

Follett promises their customers that the eBooks they buy are theirs to keep forever, though the proprietary format means access can be offered only through Follett's software (Hastings 2012). Follett is the top eBook vendor in school libraries (Whelan 2011).

CHAPTER 4

Publishers

WHO ARE THE BIG SIX?

Of course, without publishers, eBook vendors would have scant offerings for libraries. It's easy for libraries to look at publishers and see them as large, for-profit corporations that pay huge sums of money to exhibit at ALA and shower librarians and book reviewers with advanced copies of books and the occasional free drink. They seem to have all of the power in the book industry. However, publishers are seeing their industry undergo a dramatic overhaul and are working to find their way in a rapidly and radically changing market. Even the production of an eBook is fraught with difficulty. At both Digital Book World 2012 and Tools of Change 2012, two publishing conferences, the mechanics of making eBooks was a regular topic.

Producing a straight-text eBook at the same time as a print book is now a standard part of production. It gets trickier when graphics or interactive features are involved. It's also surprisingly complicated to create an eBook of an older title. Juliet Grames, senior editor at Soho Press, an independent publisher focusing on literary fiction and international crime, described the process to me. Printers typically didn't keep digital files of books in the past, and even now keep the files for only a short time, so even relatively recent titles may exist only in paper format. In Soho Press's case, they began keeping digital copies of titles in 2007, making them an early adopter of the process. For books that are not digital, they must be scanned and rendered incompletely into a text file. The files are run through software to make them text rather than images, and they end up riddled with errors. Proofreading can be outsourced for a lower cost to a compositor company, usually in India. or done in-house. Quality control, Grames emphasized, is extremely important. If a publisher puts a file with errors up online, vendors will often take it down without notifying the publisher, and getting it fixed and put back online for sale can be time consuming. All of the costs for proofreading and in-house labor for the production of an eBook are for a book that has already been edited and proofread. Once this process is done, the eBook has to be converted into various formats for the different eReaders (Grames 2012).

The more designed a book is, the more labor-intensive it is to create an eBook version of it. I asked Grames to explain what goes into typesetting a book. She said Adobe InDesign was the most commonly used software and that each page of a book is made individually. Thinking of it as text is a mistake—once a book has been typeset, changing even a single word is very expensive. The text can't easily be reflowed. Grames said "a page is a piece of art," and the text design is a part of that artwork. Even if a publisher makes something solely in eBook format, the work of the publisher, the acquisition and editorial work, are costs they have to recoup. "Books are championed by a house because they resonate," said Grames, emphasizing the passionate cultural work that publishers bring to the book business (Grames 2012). Like the contribution of libraries in championing a literate culture and creating readers, that work is often poorly understood and undervalued.

THE BIG SIX

Although publishing is not a monolithic industry, and antitrust laws keep companies from working in tandem, anyone writing or talking about the book ecosystem refers to "publishers" as a group and "the Big Six" as a special subgroup. The Big Six are the six largest publishers in the industry, and traditionally, their decisions have had a huge impact on how all publishers do business. Their influence may be changing, but they still publish a tremendous number of books. More importantly, when one of the Big Six changes how (or if) they work with libraries, that ripples through all of their imprints as well. When it comes to eBooks and libraries, that ripple effect isn't felt quite as strongly in relationships with smaller houses, but the behavior of the Big Six has a profound effect on the market. Typically, the term "indie" in publishing has applied to smaller, independent publishers (those not owned by larger publishing or media companies), but it has increasingly been used to describe self-publishing or publishing through Amazon.

Since naming the Big Six often seems like the librarian version of naming the Seven Dwarves ("Hachette, Random, HarperCollins...wait, did I already say Hachette?") I thought it might be useful to list them here, with a brief company history and a list of all their imprints as well as a few prominent authors from each house. The histories, imprints, and author names were all found on the company websites. I've also indicated if they sell eBooks to libraries, as of September 2012.

HarperCollins

HarperCollins was founded in 1817 by two brothers, James and John Harper. It was originally called J. And J. Harper, then Harper & Brothers. By 1987, it was Harper & Row, and the company was purchased by News Corporation. In 1990, News Corporation acquired William Collins & Sons, a British publisher. The two companies became HarperCollins, a worldwide publishing group ("Company Profile").

HarperCollins sells eBooks to library vendors, though as of this writing, their eBooks expire after 26 circulations.

General publishers and imprints include: Amistad, Avon, Avon Inspire, Avon Red, Broadside Books, Caedmon, Harper Design, Ecco Harper, Harper Business, Harper Luxe, Harper paperbacks, Harper Perennial, Harper Perennial Modern Classics, Harper Voyager, HarperAudio, HarperBibles, HarperCollins e-books, HarperOne, It Books, Rayo, William Morrow, and William Morrow Trade Paperbacks.

Children's publishers and imprints include: Amistad Balzer + Bray Collins, Greenwillow Books, HarperCollins Children's Audio, HarperCollins Children's Books, HarperCollins e-books, HarperFestival, HarperTeen, Katherine Tegen Books, Rayo, and Walden Pond Press.

Authors include: Meg Cabot, Michael Chabon, Janet Evanovich, Neil Gaiman, Dennis Lehane, and Mo Willems.

Penguin

In 1838, George Palmer Putnam and John Wiley formed Wiley & Putnam, a publisher and book retailer in New York, but their partnership lasted only 10 years. Putnam spun off a new firm, G. Putnam Broadway, eventually bringing his sons into the business and calling the company G. P. Putnam & Sons. By 1930, George Putnam had died, and his sons (now calling the company G. P. Putnam's Sons) had merged with another publisher, Minton, Balch & Co, with Minton and Balch running the company after Palmer C. Putnam's retirement.

Penguin Books Ltd. was formed in London in 1936, the same year that G. P. Putnam's Sons teamed up with London publisher Coward-McCann. Penguin continued to expand throughout the coming decades, with houses in Australia and Canada. By 1970, Penguin was a subsidiary of Pearson Longman Ltd. In 1975, MCA Inc. bought both the Putnam Publishing Group and its subsidiary the Berkley Publishing Group. That same year, Penguin and New York's Viking Press merged, marking Penguin's entry into the U.S. market. Both companies continued to acquire smaller publishers, especially children's presses, and in 1996, the Putnam Berkley Group was purchased by the Penguin Group. Putnam Berkley and Penguin USA formed Penguin Putnam Inc. ("History").

Penguin has recently removed their new titles from library eBook vendor's catalogs, though libraries that purchased Penguin books in the past retain access to them. In August 2012, Penguin and 3M launched a pilot project to loan eBooks to patrons at New York Public Library and Brooklyn Public Library. The publishing house will make books available to the libraries at retail pricing six months after publication and they will be licensed one year at a time. The project will be evaluated every three months and possibly rolled out to other libraries in November 2012. Since the pilot is with 3M, Penguin library books will not be available for Kindles, though that could change, as 3M has said they are pursuing Kindle compatibility and Penguin indicated they may roll out eBooks to other library vendors (Schwartz 2012b).

Adult publishers and imprints include: Ace, Alpha, Amy Einhorn Books/ Putnam, Avery, Berkley, Current, Dutton, Gotham, G. P. Putnam's Sons, HP Books, Hudson Street Press, Jeremy P. Tarcher, Jove, NAL, Pamela Dorman Books, Penguin, Penguin Press, Perigee, Plume, Portfolio, Prentice Hall Press, Riverhead, Sentinel, and Viking.

Children's publishers and imprints include: Dial, Dutton, Firebird, Frederick Warne, G. P. Putnam's Sons, Grosset & Dunlap, Philomel, Price Stern Sloan, Puffin Books, Razorbill, Speak, and Viking.

Authors include: John Sandford, Nora Roberts, Charlaine Harris, John Grisham, Geraldine Brooks, and Laurell K. Hamilton.

Macmillan

Founded by two Scottish brothers, Alexander and Daniel Macmillan, in 1843, Macmillan remained family owned until 1995, when it was purchased by Verlagsgruppe Georg von Holtzbrinck GmbH. Confusingly, there was also a New York-based publishing company Macmillan Publishing Company, created after World War II, when Macmillan sold its US company. The two Macmillans operated independently of each other and the US-based Macmillan Publishing Company went out of business in the 1990s. Macmillan's U.S. headquarters are located in the famous Flatiron building in New York City (Macmillan: A Short History).

Macmillan does not sell eBooks to libraries, but in September 2012, announced that it was working on a pilot project to sell eBooks to libraries (Albanese 2012c).

Adult trade publishers and imprints include:

Farrar, Straus & Giroux: North Point Press, Hill and Wang, Faber and Faber, Inc., First Second
Henry Holt: Metropolitan Books, Times Books, Holt Paperbacks
Macmillan Audio

Picador
St. Martin's Press: Griffen, Minotaur, St. Martin's Press Paperbacks,
    Let's Go, Thomas Dunne Books, Truman Talley Books
Tor/Forge: Starscape Tor Teen Books

Children's publishers and imprints include: Farrar, Straus, & Giroux for
Young Readers, Feiwel & Friends, Henry Holt Books for Young Readers,
Kingfisher, Priddy Books, Roaring Brook Press, and Square Fish Tor Children's.
    College and academic publishers and imprints include: Bedford Freeman
& Worth Publishing Group, Bedford/St. Martin's, Hayden-McNeil,
Palgrave Macmillan, and W. H. Freeman Worth Publishers.
    Magazines and journals include: *Nature* and *Scientific American*.
    Authors include: Hilary Mantel, Bill O'Reilly, Jeffery Archer, Augusten
Burroughs, Iris Johansen, Barbara Taylor Bradford, and Jeffery Eugenides.

Random House

Bennet Cerf and Donald Klopfer founded Random House and purchased
the Modern Library in 1925. In 1927, the two founders began publishing
other work under the Random House imprint. The company purchased publisher Alfred A. Knopf Inc. in 1960 and Pantheon Books in 1961. RCA purchased Random House in 1965, and the company bought Ballantine Books
in 1973. Advance Publications Inc. acquired Random House in 1980, and
in the subsequent years, Random House grew markedly, purchasing a number of publishing houses, including Fawcett Books in 1982 and the Crown
Publishing Group in 1988. Throughout the late 1980s and 1990s, Random
House acquired several British publishers, further expanding the company's
London operations. Random House's international operations were buoyed
when the publisher was purchased by Bertelsmann AG. Bertelsmann merged
Random House Canada with Doubleday Canada, and Bantam Books
Canada and Bertelsmann's UK branch, Transworld UK, became part of
Random House UK, which has subsidiaries in Australia, New Zealand,
and South Africa. The company also has operations in Germany, Spain,
and Latin America ("About Us").
    Random House sells eBooks to libraries, and has publicly said that they are
committed to the library market. In March 2012, the company increased the
price of their library eBooks by as much as three times the original price, with
titles available as new hardcovers selling for as much as $85 in eBook form.
The publisher sent a statement to Library Journal asking libraries for circulation data to help Random House adjust the prices of their eBooks over
time. The company's statement explained the reasoning for the price increase:
"Our guiding principles in setting these new e-prices are the unrestricted and
perpetual availability of our complete frontlist and backlist of Random House,

Inc. titles under a model of one-copy, one user. All our titles continue to be available to libraries day and date with the release of the retail edition."
Publishers and imprints include:

Crown Trade Group: Amphoto Books, Back Stage Books, Billboard Books, Broadway Books, Broadway Business, Clarkson Potter, Crown, Crown Business, Crown Forum, Doubleday Religion, Harmony Books, The Monacelli Press, Potter Craft, Potter Style, Shaye Areheart Books, Ten Speed Press, Three Rivers Press, Tricycle Press, WaterBrook Multnomah, and Watson-Guptill.
Knopf Doubleday Publishing Group: Alfred A. Knopf, Anchor Books, Doubleday, Everyman's Library, Nan A. Talese, Pantheon Books, Schocken Books, and Vintage.
Random House Publishing Group: Ballantine Books, Bantam, Delacorte, Dell, Del Ray, Del Ray/Lucas Books, The Dial Press, The Modern Library, One World, Presidio Press, Random House Trade Group, Random House Trade Paperbacks, Spectra, Spiegel & Grau, and Villard Books.
RH Audio Publishing Group: Listening Library and Random House Audio.
Random House Children's Books: Alfred A. Knopf, Bantam Beginner Books, Crown, David Fickling Books, Delacorte Press, Disney Books for Young Readers, Doubleday, Dragonfly, First Time Books, Golden Books, Landmark Books, Laurel-Leaf, Picture-backs, Random House Books for Young Readers, Robin Corey Books, Schwartz & Wade Books, Sesame Workshop, Step into Reading, Stepping Stone Books, Wendy Lamb Books, and Yearling.
RH Information Group: Fodor's Travel, Living Language, Prima Games, Princeton Review, RH Puzzles & Games, RH Reference Publishing, and Sylvan Learning.
RH International: Areté McClelland & Stewart Ltd., Plaza & Janés, RH Australia, RH of Canada Limited, RH Mondadori, RH South Africa, RH South America, RH United Kingdom, Transworld UK, and Verlagruppe RH.
RH Large Print

Authors include: Joan Didion, Gillian Flynn, Erin Morgenstern, Christopher Paolini, Dan Brown, Linda Howard, and J. Courtney Sullivan.

Simon & Schuster

In 1924, Richard L. (Dick) Simon and M. Lincoln (Max) Schuster founded Simon & Schuster, printing the first crossword puzzle book as their initial project. In 1939, the founders partnered with Robert Fair de Graff to form Pocket Books, the country's first paperback book publisher. The companies were sold to Marshall Field in 1944 and repurchased by Simon, Schuster, Leon Shimkin, and James M. Jacobson after Field died in1957. Various iterations of this group of men owned the company until 1975, when Shimkin sold it to Gulf+Western. Between 1984 and 1994, the company acquired over 60 other companies, mostly publishers of educational, professional, and reference books, like Burdett, Prentice Hall and Silver, and Macmillian Publishing Company (not to be confused with Macmillian, the Big Six publisher described here). Simon & Schuster's parent company underwent changes during this time as well. In 1989, Gulf+Western became Paramount Communications, and in 1994, the corporation was acquired by Viacom Inc. Viacom sold the educational, professional, and reference components of Simon & Schuster in 1998 to Pearson PLC. The publisher became part of the Viacom Entertainment Group in 2002, but the supervision of the company returned to Viacom's corporate headquarters in 2004. Viacom and CBS were separated into two different publicly traded companies in 2006, making Simon & Schuster part of CBS ("A Brief History of Simon & Schuster").

Simon & Schuster does not sell eBooks to libraries.

Adult publishers and imprints include: Atria, Folger Shakespeare Library, Free Press, Gallery Books, Howard Books, Pocket, Scribner, Simon & Schuster, Threshold, and Touchstone.

Children's publishers and imprints include: Aladdin, Atheneum Books for Young Readers, Beach Lane Books, Little Simon, Margaret K. McElderry Books, Paula Wiseman Books, Simon & Schuster Books for Young Readers, Simon Pulse, and Simon Spotlight.

Audio publishers and imprints include: Simon & Schuster Audio Pimsleur.

International: Simon & Schuster Australia, Simon & Schuster Canada, and Simon & Schuster UK.

Authors include: Rachael Ray, Stephen King, Jennifer Weiner, Philippa Gregory, David McCullough, and Nicole "Snooki" Polizzi.

Hachette

Little, Brown and Company was founded in 1837 and purchased by Time Inc. in 1968. Warner Communications acquired the Paperback Library and launched Warner Books in 1970. Little, Brown and Company purchased Macdonald & Co., renaming it Little, Brown and Company (UK) in 1992. By 1996, Little, Brown and Company and Warner Books merged, eventually becoming Time Warner Book Group. Throughout the 2000s, the company launched a number of imprints, specializing in a range of subjects from Christian/inspirational titles to children's books. In 2006, the company was purchased by Hachette Livre and renamed Hachette Book Group USA. By 2008, the company was called simply Hachette Book Group, and

Warner Publishing had been rechristened Grand Central Publishing ("Company History").

Hachette sold eBooks to libraries until July 2010 and then stopped making new titles available, though they have kept their backlist (through April 2010) available to libraries. There is some indication they are considering a move back into the library market (Kelley 2011d). In May 2012, Hachette announced a pilot project with two eBook distributors, but neither the libraries nor the distributors could be confirmed (Raphael 2012). In September 2012, Hachette announced that it would be raising the prices of its backlist titles through Overdrive by 104 percent, beginning October 1, 2012. The price increase has drawn strong criticism from ALA president Maureen Sullivan as well as librarians blogging about eBook issues (Price 2012), who point out that "Increasing backlist prices must either reduce the available budget for new titles or reduce acquisition of backlist titles—lost sales for Hachette either way" (Harris 2012b).

Publishers and imprints include:

Grand Central Publishing: Business Plus, Forever, GCP African American, Grand Central Life & Style, Twelve, Vision, 5 Spot.
Little, Brown and Company: Back Bay Books, Bulfinch, Mulholland Books, and Reagan Arthur Books.
FaithWords
Little, Brown and Company Books for Young Readers: Poppy LB Kids.
Center Street
Orbit
Hachette Digital
Hachette Audio
Yen Press

Authors include: Joel Osteen, James Patterson, Sherrilyn Kenyon, Christopher Buckley, Dan Rather, Kim Stanley Robinson, David Baldacci, Nicholas Sparks, and Anita Shreve.

Although the Department of Justice's lawsuit will doubtless have tremendous impact on the retail eBook market, it remains to be seen if it will change any library-related policies for publishers. Smaller publishers have not yet started experimenting with library sales models. Most either sell eBooks to libraries or don't at all. Scholastic's decision to sell Harry Potter eBooks without DRM (or with very lightweight DRM, depending on your view of watermarking) and allow libraries to loan them (with DRM) through OverDrive has received attention and may signal a change in how publishers sell eBooks. It can be tiresome to hear, but the situation is complicated and seems to simultaneously change constantly and not at all. We're always waiting for some kind of resolution, and we may be waiting for quite some time. The "before" and "after" of eBooks may not be resolved or be obvious for quite some time, especially when it comes to library lending. In an interview for Tools of Change 2012, publishing startup maven and coeditor of *Book: A Futurist's Manifesto* Hugh McGuire said that while publishing had a decent handle on the production of eBooks, it was not prepared for the " 'digital-native disruption.' What happens when all new books are ebooks, and the majority of books are read on digital devices, most of which are connected to the Internet?" (Webb 2012, 12). McGuire added that this shift "brings with it so many new expectations from consumers, and I think this is where the real disruption in the market will come" (Webb 2012, 12). In other words, we ain't seen nothing yet.

PUBLISHERS AND LIBRARY ACCESS

At one of my very first library jobs, there was a book order meeting once a week. We would go through that week's book review media and decide what to buy for the library. At the end of the meeting, we'd look at patron requests. The more senior librarians always checked the name of the publisher of the patron requests, trying to weed out any titles from "vanity publishers." The unstated policy was that we would buy things only from "real" publishers. Yet I used to scoff (quietly, to myself) at book request forms that included publisher. Readers rarely seemed to know or care who had published a book, unless it was a travel book a romance (Harlequin has an impressive relationship with their readers) or published by a company that featured the publisher name prominently on the cover (DK books spring to mind).

When it comes to eBooks, of course, publishers matter much more. The consortium I work for offers eBooks and eAudiobooks through popular library eBook vendor OverDrive to its libraries, and shortly after one of our smallest libraries signed up, the director IMed me saying she wasn't thrilled by the selection. I reminded her that Simon & Schuster, Hachette, and Macmillian don't offer eBooks through OverDrive and that our OverDrive libraries had decided not to buy HarperCollins books. Memory jogged, she realized that yes, that was what was off about the collection. Although publishers don't make decisions together because of antitrust laws, we tend to view them as a monolithic industry. The Big Six are not always representative of the industry at large, and in the eBook world, they have very different policies.

In February of 2011, OverDrive announced that one publisher's eBooks would expire from library collections after 26 circulations. HarperCollins was swiftly identified as the publishing house in question. After librarians protested online, including a call to boycott HarperCollins eBooks, OverDrive moved HarperCollins titles to their own section of their eBook marketplace, so librarians who did not want to buy eBooks that would expire could avoid them entirely. HarperCollins responded, saying that "twenty-six circulations can provide a year of availability for titles with the highest demand, and much longer for other titles and core backlist. If a library decides to repurchase an e-book later in the book's life, the price will be significantly lower as it will be pegged to a paperback price point. Our hope is to make the cost per circulation for e-books less than that of the corresponding physical book. In fact, the digital list price is generally 20% lower than the print version, and sold to distributors at a discount" (Hadro and Fialkoff 2011).

However, for many librarians the issue wasn't the number of circulations, but ownership. eBooks are not purchased, but rather licensed, often at a higher cost than print books. Salt Lake City's library told the *Deseret News* that the library pays more for eBooks of most titles (Ferguson 2011). While most librarians are sympathetic to the problem publishers face with immortal eBooks, buying a book with planned obsolescence built in isn't economically feasible for most cash-strapped organizations. As it is, libraries do not own their eBooks the same way they own their print books, a point that was highlighted by another publisher in 2011.

In November of 2011, library patrons who had holds on Penguin titles found that when their turn came up, they were unable to check out a Kindle edition, though the Kindle edition had been previously available. Penguin had contacted OverDrive and asked them to remove new Penguin titles and to disable Kindle access for their titles. OverDrive complied, but no announcement was made until after many libraries received complaints from patrons (Kelley 2011f). After the uproar, Penguin agreed to reinstate Kindle access to their titles until the end of 2011, but new Penguin titles will still be unavailable.

For front-line librarians, explaining a publisher-based access model is a headache. A patron looking for a *New York Times* Notable book probably doesn't know (or care) whom it was published by. The publishers' ability to remove access means libraries cannot be sure of what their collection is. Collection has long been at the heart of the library. Libraries and their collections are one of the few remaining commons in public life.

In *All That We Share: A Field Guide to the Commons*, Jay Walljasper explores the idea of the commons and the dangers of excessive privatization in modern life. The chapter on the library discusses the library as a physical space, as a community commons where citizens can have meetings, friends can run into each other, and community leaders can post notices (Walljasper 2010, 148–52). While the community living room aspect of libraries is vital, the cultural commons that the collection represents is an important one. Each library's collection represents the life of the mind in its community.

Although libraries generally do not wish to track the reading habits of their patrons, when we stumble across historic data we delight in exploring the bookish pursuits of our predecessors (Trubek 2011). The What Middletown Read database provides access to the circulation records of the Muncie Public Library in Indiana from 1891 to 1902, and researchers and journalists alike have delighted in discovering what readers of the past enjoyed (Plotz 2011). The collection and how it is used are valuable components of the commons of the library.

If a library does not own its collection, what does that mean for the commons? What does it mean for the integrity of the content in that collection? In *Searcher* magazine, Charles Hamaker cited Random House's licensing language that asserts the publisher's right to make changes to the content of an eBook at any time. "The ability to modify the published text without notification, tracking, versioning, archiving, or any other means that might provide the original text for readers is destructive to the tradition of the history of the printed word and the tradition of Western scholarship. If we want to know what Galileo wrote, we can still go back to the original text. What if the Catholic Church had had the potential to wipe out completely the record of its writings?" (Hamaker 2011). This concern is shared by Nicholas Carr, who wrote in the *Wall Street Journal* that the printing press brought a "new set of literary workers coalesced in publishing houses, collaborating with writers to perfect texts before they went on press. The verb 'to finalize' became common in literary circles, expressing the permanence of printed words. Different editions still had textual variations, introduced either intentionally as revisions or inadvertently through sloppy editing or typesetting, but books still came to be viewed, by writer and reader alike, as immutable objects. They were written for posterity" (N. Carr 2011). Both Carr and Hamaker are concerned about abuses possible when text can so easily be manipulated. Carr speculates that school boards could command a greater influence over what students read, going so far as to edit books with local biases and prejudices. Hamaker wonders about undue influence of government or nongovernment entities, noting that while book challenges are common now, they do not come with the ability to remove the offending passages of a book. Carr posits that, more than governmental interference, "what may be more insidious is the pressure to fiddle with books for commercial reasons. Because e-Readers gather enormously detailed information on the way people read, publishers may soon be awash in market research ... What will be lost, or at least diminished, is the sense of a book as a finished and complete object, a self-contained work of art" (N. Carr 2011). Hamaker concludes that "we cannot as a civilization permit our complainers' and dreamers' and thinkers' words to be destroyed by the simple expedient of the ability to 'replace, edit or modify the contents' of any ebook" (Hamaker 2011).

eBooks, as discussed earlier, are destined to evolve and become quite different from their printed counterparts. Their very digital nature and potential to be used in new ways makes them different. We are accustomed to past knowledge remaining at least somewhat frozen in time for us to peruse, but perhaps that's not inherent to knowledge, but rather an accident of the technology available at the time. Discussing his newest book, *Too Big to Know*, with *Library Journal*'s Barbara Fister, David Weinberger said, "Paper-based knowledge succeeded when it settled matters, that is, when it drove out difference. It drove it underground, marginalized it, made it invisible. But networks only have value when there is disagreement and difference, and as networks, those differences are now linked" (Fister 2012). Weinberger sees the value in academic journals filtering submitted articles, but adds that if those journals are available only to the elite few, the social cost of that added value is too high (Fister 2012).

In his (tellingly) book, Weinberger says that just because we produce so much digitally doesn't mean we'll be forever running back, editing our mistakes out. But we won't be reliant on books in the same way, either. In his review of *Too Big to Know*, Jeff Jarvis says that Weinberger has "profoundly disruptive ideas about ideas" (Jarvis 2012). Knowledge is now larger than we are, than our brains and institutions and paper books are. "Knowledge becomes the province of the network" (Jarvis 2012) and is no longer a singular body that one can master or even comprehend. Perhaps eBooks are inherently a part of that network in a way that print books are not. Publishers and authors can and perhaps will revoke access, make changes, and in other ways alter an eBook in ways they cannot in paper, but they may be fighting a futile battle against the evolution of knowledge. "If books taught us that knowledge is a long walk from A to Z, the networking of knowledge may be teaching us the world itself is more like a shapeless, intertwingled, unmasterable web than like a well-reasoned argument" (Weinberger 2011, 119).

WHAT DO PUBLISHERS PLAN TO DO WITH EBOOKS?

That revolution in how we know things and how we understand and process knowledge (and what counts as knowledge, even) can seem abstract and distant to librarians teaching people how to use the mouse or set up eMail. But it's part of what leaves most people who work with books with the feeling that long-held truths are being upended. Yet eBook skepticism is not without some merit. While it's clear that for many readers, eBooks have firmly taken hold, this is not the first time we've heard about the coming eBook revolution.

Many librarians will remember the initial surge of interest in eBooks in the late 90s and early 2000s. Indeed, many libraries began purchasing eBooks when NetLibrary started offering them in 1999, and when Over-Drive came on the library scene in 2002. While librarians may or may not have seen this as the early rumblings of a move to entirely electronic books, for publishers, this was the first wave of eBook speculation and occasional panic. Publishers were spending money on potential eBook solutions and being exhorted to think about the digital future throughout the mid-1990s (Thompson 2010, 312). Larger publishing houses were exhorted to take the lead, lest smaller, more nimble companies leap to the fore, eclipsing them in the digital future to come (Thompson 2010, 313).

Reports from organizations like PricewaterhouseCoopers and Arthur Andersen predicted that eBooks would be anywhere from 10 to 17 percent of the market and spending would be in the billions by 2005. In 2000, Stephen King's successful novella *Riding the Bullet* was sold electronically and saw 400,000 downloads in the first 24 hours. By 2001, however, it was clear that these predictions were overeager (Thompson 2010, 313).

eBooks are arguably even more disruptive for publishers than they are for libraries. Publishers face not only an upheaval in the sale and distribution of their books, but they must also contend with an entirely new marketplace. Self-publishing, once relegated to "vanity" presses, has experienced something of a renaissance as eBooks increase in popularity. Authors like Amanda Hocking and J. A. Konrath have made headlines with their surprisingly large paychecks generated by self-publishing on Amazon. Million-dollar paydays are not the rule in publishing, self- or otherwise, and Amanda Hocking has since signed with St. Martin's Press, but some of the more successful self-published authors, most notably J. A. Konrath, have been outspoken in their criticism of the publishing industry. Publishers, meanwhile, are responding not as a monolithic industry, but individually, making it very hard to say what publishing plans to do about eBooks.

In a talk entitled "The Opportunity in Abundance," publishing consultant Brian O'Leary exhorted publishers at the 2011 Books in Browsers conference to work with everyone in the book ecosystem to redefine the industry. He cited the danger in short-term thinking, saying that "focusing on our immediate needs risks the loss of a significant supply chain cog—libraries, wholesalers and retailers included. In the current, complex system, we don't fully understand the value added by each of these partners. Losing them can and does create a set of unintended consequences." O'Leary cites Peter Brantley's talk from the Firebrand Community Conference in 2010, saying that publishers are trying to extend agreements from an earlier era, despite the massive upheaval to their business (Brantley 2010). O'Leary reminds his audience that "abundance hasn't quite gutted the old rules, but it has rendered them inadequate." His solution is a new approach to negotiations in the publishing industry: "Using serial negotiations between two parties makes it impossible to revamp our supply chains so we can respond to content abundance. What we need is a new approach: many parties, negotiating many issues simultaneously" (O'Leary 2011).

Content abundance, says O'Leary, forces publishers to face their weaknesses, but also has serious implications for everyone connected to publishing, including libraries. O'Leary cites four implications of abundance: a need for open, accessible, and interoperable content; a focus on context-based discovery; the encouragement of broader use of content; and the creation of tools for readers to help them manage abundance (O'Leary 2011).

He invokes the vision of Michael Hart, founder of Project Gutenberg who thought that the average middle-class reader would have a portable device capable of holding a petabyte of material by 2021. In 2011, 15 percent of people in the United States owned an eReader, which is an enormous percentage of regular readers. The heaviest readers are often eBook buyers. Mike Shatzkin predicts that future devices will be cheap and ubiquitous, with a fire hose of free content built in to people's basic cable subscription (Shatzkin 2011f).

While we are not privy to the long-range plans of publishers, it is clear that publishers and those who work with them are looking into the future with some optimism tempered not by fear but by pragmatism. In her summary of Digital Book World 2012, *Library Journal*'s Heather McCormack observed a change in the attitude of publishing executives, noting that "the damaging fear-induced myopia" (McCormack 2012) of previous years was receding. She added that although the term "ecosystem" was not widely used in years past, "at Digital Book World . . . I heard more than one CEO use it, along with independent booksellers, it must be noted. The word, of course, encapsulates what librarians and library advocates have long argued for in the digital wars—capitalism that supports *anyone* with a stake in information and encourages fluid tiers of access. Or, if you will, a most beatific 'United Nations of Reading,' to quote Eric Hellman, who was inspired last fall by Brian O'Leary's excellent Books in Browers presentation, 'The Opportunity in Abundance' " (McCormack 2012).

As the eBook frontier becomes a less wild and terrifying place for publishers, will more publishers be willing to partner with libraries?

WHY DO PUBLISHERS TREAT EBOOKS DIFFERENTLY?

Publishers and Pricing

Stop me if you've heard this one: eBooks are a disruptive technology. We keep hearing that because it's true. eBooks challenge all aspects of the book ecosystem—publishers, authors, readers, and librarians are changing how they produce, distribute, lend, and consume the written word. This is what Mike Shatzkin calls an "existential crisis for the twentieth century book industry. No one escapes and the solutions are not going to look like the present day" (Shatzkin 2011f). Right now, the infrastructure of publishing and distribution is still devoted to books on shelves; though it's getting harder to justify the costs of print, publishers can't abandon it, since it's still most of book communication (Shatzkin 2011f).

Libraries are increasingly concerned about the role Amazon plays in the eBook marketplace. Until recently, libraries couldn't offer eBooks for the Kindle, which made our patrons unhappy. Once OverDrive partnered with Amazon to offer library eBooks for the Kindle, librarians were displeased when Amazon's expiration notices offered the option to buy the eBook from Amazon. Amazon makes libraries nervous, but it's nothing compared to how publishers feel about the behemoth.

It's important to bear in mind that although we talk about publishing as a monolithic industry, it really isn't. I've focused on commercial publishing and emphasized the actions of the Big Six, but the industry is much more complex than that. If you're interested in getting more insight into publishing, there are a number of fascinating blogs from those who work at, in, and with publishers:

Brian O'Leary of Magellan Media blogs about publishing issues, and touches on libraries regularly: http://www.magellanmediapartners.com/index.php/

Mike Shatzkin of the Idea Logical Company, another industry consultant with an active blog: http://www.idealog.com/

LJNDawson works in the book industry and blogs about ISBNs, standards, and metadata, with the occasional personal entry thrown in: http://ljndawson.wordpress.com/

Melville House, an independent publisher, has an excellent blog: http://mhpbooks.com/.

Peter Brantley's contributions to *Publishers Weekly*'s PWxyz blog offer excellent library-related insights into the world of eBooks: http://blogs.publishersweekly.com/blogs/PWxyz/.

There are also a number of publishing websites and publications:

Many librarians already read Publishers Weekly: http://www.publishersweekly.com.

Publishing Perspectives also offers news, focusing on international publishing: http://publishingperspectives.com/.

Digital Book World focuses on digital publishing and eBooks: http://www.digitalbookworld.com/.

PaidContent looks at digital content a little more broadly, with an emphasis on the economic side of things: http://paidcontent.org/.

Publishers are hoping that Kobo, Barnes & Noble, and Apple can continue to compete with Amazon. Each sale has become vital in the eBook market, a challenge that print did not face (Shatzkin 2011f). A reader who buys books from Amazon also borrows from the library and also buys books from bookstores (large and possibly independent), but a reader who owns a Kindle is getting eContent only from Amazon (although the Verso Advertising survey found that avid readers split their purchases between various retailers) (Verso Digital 2011).

Amazon has also shown that people buying eBooks are willing to choose from the 99¢ bin and eschew content from large publishing houses entirely. As far as the publishing industry is concerned, eBooks are potentially changing reader behavior. Retailers are publisher's biggest stakeholders, and Amazon is an enormous threat to bookstores of all stripes. The company is so large, it can afford to subsidize sales of best sellers, possibly going so far as to take a $20 hit on some titles (Shatzkin 2011a).

Pricing has been a sore subject between publishers and Amazon since the introduction of the Kindle. In order to drive demand for the Kindle after its initial release, Amazon sold bestsellers for $9.99, taking a $2 to $3 loss on each sale. Their willingness and financial ability to sell eBooks at a loss troubled publishers, who feared Amazon would forever be the only eBook game in town. When Apple introduced the iPad, they offered a different model to the publishers. Instead of selling eBooks wholesale to Apple, publishers set the price for a book, and gave Apple a 30 percent commission on each sale (Levine 2011, 159–60).

In 2010, Macmillan and Amazon executives met and the publisher asked Amazon to agree to the agency-pricing model, with Macmillan setting the price of each eBook. If Amazon refused, Macmillan planned to delay the release of eBook editions of some forthcoming titles. Amazon responded by removing the "buy" buttons from Macmillan's print and eBooks (Levine 2011, 160–61). Within a few days, however, Amazon capitulated, noting that Macmillan "has a monopoly over their own titles" (Levine 2011, 161). Shortly thereafter, Simon & Schuster, HarperCollins, Penguin, and Hachette all announced that they would be selling to Amazon using agency pricing as well (though each company had to hammer out the details of the deal with Amazon). Random House followed suit in early 2011 (Levine 2011, 161). It's worth noting that even Amazon had to acknowledge the power publishers have when it comes to content.

Agency pricing is not about money, at least not in the sense of making more of it. Publishers make less money with agency pricing. Wholesale eBooks were bringing in $12 or $13 each, while agency-priced eBooks might retail for $13 with $9 going back to the publisher (Levine 2011, 161). Higher prices also mean fewer sales, but that's not what the publishers were worried about. They feared eBooks so cheap that the only real money to be made would be in selling the gadgets, as well as Amazon's lock on the eReader (and therefore eBook) market (Levine 2011, 159).

Publishers, like libraries, are caught between two worlds. Producing, marketing, and selling eBooks is very different from producing, marketing, and selling print books. At Digital Book World 2012, attendees were exhorted by more than one speaker to develop relationships with readers and reader communities, and "verticalization" was stressed. In the case of publishing, this means marketing to audiences based on areas of interest, rather than the traditional publishing focus on individual titles (Shatzkin 2012c). Readers behave differently in an eBook market, and eBooks behave differently than print books. For publishers, the changed behavior of the consumer is of tremendous importance. For librarians, the limitations placed on library eBooks have taken center stage. Which is not to say that publishers aren't interested in eBooks' unique properties or that librarians shouldn't care about consumer or patron behavior. Far from it, but right now our relationship with digital books is centered on the current eBook purchasing and circulation environment, and all of the issues that environment creates.

CHAPTER 5

Issues

DISCOVERABILITY AND THE VALUE OF LIBRARIES

How do publishers view libraries? There are likely as many answers as there are publishers. At OverDrive's 2011 Digipalooza conference, Ruth Liebmann of Random House praised libraries effusively. Liebmann touted libraries as focal points of their communities and said that the connection to readers is valuable. Most book sales still come from word of mouth and libraries are word-of-mouth engines, connecting readers with books every hour they're open. Libraries connect readers to books without turning a profit. They are purely focused on the books themselves, which is a valuable perspective for publishers.

eBooks have provoked a lot of existential angst among librarians. Publishers have also found themselves in an anxiety-producing position with the advent of wildly popular eBooks and online self-publishing. Writerly success is rare, no matter how one is published, but a number of Amazon-powered authors regularly lambast "big publishing" for clinging to out-of-date models and business practices in order to retain their power in the book ecosystem. As you might expect, publishers find this characterization insulting and inaccurate, though many publishers have been slow to adapt to the changing market.

Publishers, very much like libraries, contribute to the world of books and book culture in intangible ways. Of course, the physical books themselves have come from publishers, but the selection, editing, and marketing (to name a few areas of publishing expertise) that publishing houses do may go largely unnoticed by the reading public. Just as librarians find themselves asking "how can we put a price on a literate populace?," publishers wonder how to express the value of the commitment they make to their authors and their books.

Libraries are places of discovery—people become readers in the library, readers become fans of new books and authors, and fans buy more books. In *Library Journal*, Madeline McIntosh, the president of sales, operations, and digital for Random House, said that publishers "understand the pressure that librarians are under, and we want to work with you" (Sheehan 2011). However, she added that "we also want to be honest about the fact that for us, the heart of what makes a library important is defined by physical books, in a physical space, connected to its community by face-to-face relationships and coming together in person over books. The value of a library to us—and our authors—is inextricably linked to a library having a physical space, where people can come and discover books" (Sheehan 2011).

Some librarians took some issue with the emphasis on physical books as a defining characteristic of the library. That is certainly still the case, but libraries are allocating more space to patrons for studying, coworking, gathering together, and participating in library and community programs. While many people, including people working in the book industry, see libraries as book temples, I believe that McIntosh's concern is not that the library be a glorified warehouse of codexes, but rather a place for discovery.

Publishers, librarians, and readers alike struggle with online discovery. Online tools are made largely for finding, and have yet to replicate the casual serendipity of wandering around a bookstore or library. Samples are helpful, but not quite the same as flipping through a book; in an eBook world, "the chance of making a random, genuine discovery is nothing but time consuming" (Nawotka 2010). Discovery in the physical realm is understood by readers, librarians, publishers, and booksellers. Displays and hand selling are art forms that don't translate well to the eBook realm. A reader can walk up to a table full of books, but still usually has to search for an eBook.

Douglas County Libraries (Colorado) have implemented an innovative solution to encourage browsing of both physical and virtual collections. Their "powerwalls" are attention-grabbing displays of books that account for 60 percent of the system's print circulation (Sendze 2011). Adjacent to the powerwalls are large touch screens that allow patrons to browse, search, and check out eBooks. Library members have a single "My Account" log-in, with sections for physical and eContent checkouts. Their accounts can be connected to Facebook, to allow readers to share what they're enjoying and get recommendations from friends. Douglas County has also developed an app that mirrors the powerwall in the library (Sendze 2011).

Discoverability matters to publishers and to librarians. It matters to readers, but perhaps not as much as ease of use does. Columbus Metropolitan Library (CML) surveyed their inactive and light users to see if they were using the library's eBook collection. Twenty-one percent said they were not using library eBooks and had no plans to do so in the future, but according to Alison Circle, CML's director of marketing, a large percentage also indicated that they were very likely to try the library's eBooks if there were easy and convenient ways to download them (Circle 2011).

Still, "discovery" is a watchword in the publishing industry. It's something libraries do as a matter of course, in the physical world. Slate's tech columnist Farhad Manjoo wrote a column arguing that we should let indie bookstores close and just buy our books on Amazon (I like his tech columns, but maybe I don't want to talk books with him). He was, of course, roundly condemned by authors and booksellers alike. But he made some interesting assertions about discovery. Specifically, he claimed that "a physical store . . . offers a relatively paltry selection, no customer reviews, no reliable way to find what you're looking for, and a dubious recommendations engine. Amazon suggests books based on others you've read; your local store recommends what the employees like. If you don't choose your movies based on what the guy at the box office recommends, why would you choose your books that way?" (Manjoo 2011).

I'm not even going to get into the difference between the "guy at the box office" and a dedicated bookseller or librarian (though I would not be surprised to find serious film buffs slinging popcorn at an indie theater). But Amazon's recommendations are just not that good. First of all, it doesn't recommend based on what we've read. It recommends based on what we buy, and while there is a way to edit our purchase history to indicate which items were gifts and which weren't, most consumers aren't likely to take the time to edit their own metadata so Amazon can know even more about them. Really good book recommendations come from the relationships we build with other readers, whether they're friends, librarians, or booksellers. Even online, sites like LibraryThing create better recommendations, because they're based on what people have read and rated. Manjoo is right that Amazon has everything under the sun, but that isn't the be-all and end-all of discovery. When libraries weed, circulation improves, because editing helps people see what's there. Verso Advertising's survey of book-buying behaviors found that only 16 percent of readers said they discovered new titles via online algorithm, while 49 percent said they relied on personal recommendations and 31 percent said they looked to bookstore staff for recommendations (Verso Digital 2011). That's a huge vote for talking to other people to get book recommendations. I was on a panel about libraries and discovery at Digital Book World 2012 and I told the audience that every time I searched for a pregnancy related book on Amazon, it suggested a particular book about pregnancy that was, to a human, obviously not what I was interested in. I was interested in factual books written by doctors and Amazon repeatedly suggested a book of essays written by a minor celebrity. It was the sort of recommendation that a person, especially someone who did any kind of reader's advisory would not make. It in no way aided discovery for me, and I had a much easier time finding books at libraries and bookstores. At their best, Amazon's suggestions are okay, but they rarely compare to a friend pressing a much-loved paperback into your hand, or a librarian engaging a patron in discussion about what she likes to read and making well-reasoned recommendations. I'm waxing anecdotal here, but good recommendations are hard to quantify.

All of this grousing about Amazon's recommendations shows us is that online discovery is hard. Amazon has enormous resources to make online discovery work and it's still not as good as a person can be. This isn't a problem librarians have to solve on their own, but it is an area of great interest to publishers. Libraries are only just starting to get recognition as serious channels of discovery. Strangely, Amazon may turn out to be an inadvertent advocate for libraries. At Digital Book World 2012, Amazon vice president for Kindle content Russ Grandinetti extolled the virtues of lending as a way of driving book sales. Lending and selling have always been separate business, but by bringing them together, Amazon could prove the importance of libraries to publishing's livelihood.

VENDOR DEPENDENCE: HOW DO WE CHART OUR OWN PATH?

Historically, libraries have purchased physical objects, because that's how information came: bound in paper. Things started getting murkier with database subscriptions. We purchase access, but if the costs rise beyond the library's means, access to everything including back issues is lost. With eBooks, things have taken a truly strange turn. We buy the books, in electronic format, but the access to them is mediated by a third party. If that third party goes out of business or sells their eBook division, we now potentially own books we can't get to.

Electronically, libraries are still very dependent on vendors. The Connecticut State Library purchased an eAudiobook collection from Ingram. Titles were purchased from Ingram, and the patron interface was managed by Ingram. In July 2011, Ingram told the State Library that the platform for access would be turned over to Recorded Books. The library was still able to purchase eAudiobooks from Ingram, but the access would now be mediated by another company.

The State Library had very carefully negotiated the original contract with Ingram. The library owned the content they were purchasing and paid an annual fee for access. However, without access, ownership is relatively meaningless. The contract contained a stipulation that if Ingram went out of business, the library could download all of its purchased content in order to migrate it to another vendor's platform.

The vendor's proposed cost for access to the titles on the new access platform was significantly higher than it had been with Ingram, and Recorded Books did not promise ownership of titles purchased from them going forward. The ownership of the original collection of titles came into question. The State Library had purchased them from Ingram under one agreement, but was now accessing them through Recorded Books under a different agreement. While the items are available for download, the State Library continues to negotiate with Recorded Books over the ownership issue.

Although this story did not result in a Kansas-style showdown between library and vendor, it does illustrate both the problems of unclear ownership and the issue of vendor dependence. If the Kansas state librarian had refused to sign the new contract with OverDrive but was unable to move the state's eBooks to 3M, would the library still own those eBooks? How would they provide access to them? Douglas County Library in Colorado has developed a way to own some of their eBooks, but it requires negotiation with publishers, and so far they've been most successful with Colorado independent publishers. But even moving their eBooks from one vendor platform to another required Kansas to contact each publisher individually (Kelley 2011e).

Managing our own vendor negotiations is something best done at least somewhat collectively. Consortia and large systems are the most likely candidates to handle that kind of legal legwork. Even then, outside legal assistance is advisable. The appeal of vendors is undeniable, and for many libraries, they may be the best or the only option available. Libraries have always worked with vendors to purchase content and provide access to electronic materials. None of this is to suggest a Jets-versus-Sharks-style rumble between libraries and vendors. But what we're usually aiming for when we sign up with a vendor is a partnership. Right now, with eBooks the scales are always tipped. If we invest in content on one platform, we may or may not be able to move it to another. We may or may not have ownership of the content we purchase. Academic librarians have been very vocal in their frustrations at vendor dependence in the electronic journal market. Public librarians are on the path to that same frustration.

PRICING

Right now, the library eBook market is in flux. Pricing varies widely, and as we negotiate our position with vendors and publishers, pricing is often at the center of the conversation. Vendor fees and structure are not consistent, but it's publisher pricing that gets the most attention. HarperCollins and Random House are the only two of the Big Six publishers that (as of this writing and excluding pilot projects) sell eBooks to library vendors. However, each has developed a pricing structure that breaks from the earlier model of treating eBooks somewhat like print books. The disparate prices have been very clearly illustrated by Douglas County Libraries' charts that show the differences between the consumer and library markets by listing prices for *New York Times* best sellers through library vendors and bookstores, a move that has grabbed attention from their local politicians (Price 2012).

eBooks generally do not come with the same discounts that libraries enjoy on print books. Theoretically, they do not require the processing and usually come with MARC records, so adding them to the catalog is a faster (and therefore cheaper) process. However, they take a relatively large bite out of dwindling book budgets. For the two largest publishers that sell to libraries, that bite has gotten even larger. HarperCollins's pricing structure has kept the price of eBooks the same, but requires libraries to rebuy a title after it has circulated 26 times. Random House is pursuing the opposite strategy. They're explicitly promising ownership of titles purchased (Maier 2012), but charging significantly more for each title. Ownership, in this case, revolves around the ability to take the titles to a different platform. Christopher Harris asked if we can ILL titles or sell them at used-book sales (Maier 2012). For now, those options aren't being explicitly addressed and, indeed, we do not have a technological mechanism for carrying out either option with eBooks.

Refusal to buy eBooks with unsustainable pricing structure has been a common response. When HarperCollins announced their 26-circulations limitation, many called for a boycott. Though I agreed with the idea of not buying HarperCollins eBooks, I have come to think that "boycott" was not the right word. It conjures images of people marching in the streets, chanting about unfair practices, when I saw the decision not to buy HarperCollins eBooks more as a financial choice—libraries and consortia with shrinking budgets can't afford books that don't last. The reaction to the Random House pricing has been more subdued. Random's pricing change comes over a year after the HarperCollins decision, and the hue and cry that went up after that has not changed their policy. Also, Random House has offered ownership, which was what librarians said they wanted after the HarperCollins decision, and expressed a willingness to work with libraries to find prices that everyone can live with. Still, at least two groups of libraries have declared moratoriums on Random House eBooks. Libraries Online Incorporated (LION), a group of 25 public, school, and academic libraries in Connecticut, and the South Shore Public Libraries in Nova Scotia, Canada, announced they would not buy Random House eBooks (Kelley 2012a). In LION's case, the board also encouraged its members to consider eschewing Random's print titles as well (Libraries Online, Inc).

Many librarians (myself included) would like to see a tiered pricing structure from publishers. For some titles, ownership may be a worthwhile investment. For others (I am writing this at the height of *50 Shades of Grey* mania), ownership of every single copy purchased may not be critical. A tiered model that allows for ownership at one end and rental at the other might satisfy both librarian and publisher needs.

Don't forget that there are quite a few resources for free eBooks. If you're just getting started at your library with eBooks, offering free eBooks can help you gauge interest in digital content in your community. Your library may be scrambling to catch up with a tech-savvy population or you may be leading the way. Pointing your patrons at free eBooks can help you find out where you stand.

Project Gutenberg: http://www.gutenberg.org/
The Internet Archive's Open Library: http://openlibrary.org/ (http://archive
     .org/ also has free music, moving images, and audio recordings)
HathiTrust: http://www.hathitrust.org/ (the content tends to be more
     academic and usually has to be read on a computer screen, but it's a
     fun site to browse)

Department of Justice and Pricing

Pricing is not just an issue in libraries. Retail pricing has made headlines with the Department of Justice's (DOJ) lawsuit against Apple and five of the Big Six publishers. The DoJ and an ever-increasing number of states are alleging that Apple, Penguin, Macmillan, Simon & Schuster, Hachette, and HarperCollins worked together to fix prices of eBooks. Simon & Schuster, Hachette, and HarperCollins settled with the DOJ shortly after the suit was filed, and will amend their agency arrangements. However, Apple, Penguin, and Macmillan are fighting the allegations. Their motion to dismiss was denied, and the case will move forward. The outcome of this case will have huge implications for the book industry. The information pouring out of the lawsuit has been illuminating, including evidence of conversations about windowing, the practice of delaying eBook releases of new titles. The suit also alleges that Macmillan CEO John Sargent asked Apple to take a smaller cut from new releases because the agency-pricing model was actually decreasing revenues for the publishers (Litte 2012).

In September 2012, on the same day Amazon announced their new Kindle devices, a federal judge approved the settlement terms agreed to by Amazon, Hachette, Simon & Schuster, and HarperCollins (Bosman 2012c). The settlement brought about swift changes in pricing for consumer ebooks. HarperCollins forged new contracts with retailers right away and its titles were discounted on Amazon, though the publisher raised the list price of some titles to compensate for the loss (Owen 2012d). Still under considera-tion are small refunds to consumers who purchased eBooks, though it seems likely that, if approved, those refunds will not make their way to people's wallets for quite some time (Roberts 2012).

As Mike Shatzkin put it, right now this lawsuit means "Amazon (which includes any other player largely dependent on Amazon) and the most

By the time you're reading this, the lawsuit will have progressed and may even be over. It's not hard to find coverage of the DOJ's suit against Apple, Macmillan, and Penguin. The *New York Times*, *Wired* magazine, NPR's *On the Media*, CNET, and other major publications have been covering it. However, for in-depth analysis and coverage by industry experts, I've been following these three writers:

Jane Litte of DearAuthor.com, a romance review site with regular posts about eBooks. Litte wrote a much-cited primer on the lawsuit: http://dearauthor.com/ebooks/antitrust-primer-for-the-publishing-price-fixing-lawsuit/.
Laura Hazard Owen of paidcontent.org, a site devoted to "the economics of digital content." Her article, "Everything You Need to Know about the E-book Lawsuit in One Post," explains the various pricing models and reactions from the major players: http://paidcontent.org/2012/04/11/everything-you-need-to-know-about-e-book-doj-lawsuit-in-one-post/.
Mike Shatzkin of the Idealogical company, a publishing consultant who blogs at idealog.com. His posts include some speculation, prognostication, and intense discussion in the comments: http://www.idealog.com/.

price-conscious ebook consumers have won. Everybody else in the ecosystem: authors, publishers, and other vendors, have lost. The reaction from all quarters seems to confirm that analysis" (Shatzkin 2012a). Laura Hazard Owen, who covers the case for paidcontent.org, cites commentary from industry analysts, authors, and booksellers saying that a publisher's best strategy might be to drop DRM, which would allow customers to break from the closed Kindle ecosystem (Owen 2012b).

PIRACY

The Harry Potter series has yet to be released in eBook form. J. K. Rowling has launched a website, Pottermore, that will eventually distribute the series in digital form, with each copy carrying a distinct digital watermark meant to discourage piracy (Messieh 2011). But a quick search on Google turns up sites offering the books in PDF, ePub, plain text, and more. While sharing a book collection isn't quite as easy as sharing a music collection, people are willing to scan books and make them available online. The comparison with music has a long reach in the eBook world, with consumers using the experience of ripping their own CDs to an Mp3 player to justify downloading pirated copies of books they already own.

The Verso Advertising study asked tablet and eReader owners how many times in the last year they had downloaded an eBook file from an "online file storage service such as RapidShare, Megaupload, Hotfile, etc." According to the 2011 survey, 12.5 percent said 1 or 2, 7.5 percent said 3 or 4, 5.9 percent said 5 to 9, 7.3 percent said 10 or more, and a surprising 10.6 percent said they weren't sure. When looking at men aged 18 to 34, the percentage of people confessing to some piracy increased somewhat, with over 40 percent saying they had pirated books that year, 44 percent saying they hadn't, and 16 percent declining to answer the question (Verso Digital).

A British survey conducted in the spring of 2011 found that 29 percent of eReader owners and 36 percent of tablet owners willingly admitted to ebook piracy. For women over 35, the number was 12 percent, compared to 5 percent of the same demographic who said they had downloaded pirated music (Williams 2011). Shifts in behavior like that are what leave publishers concerned that the ebook market is truly uncharted territory.

eBook piracy is either a crisis or no big deal, depending on who you ask. Studies on piracy often cite wildly high numbers, which are often overblown, as eBook blogger Eric Hellman has shown in a series of posts from 2010 (Hellman 2010a), coming to the conclusion that searches for pirated ebooks number only in the tens of thousands worldwide (Hellman 2010b). Numbers aside, many assert that piracy is not a problem, regardless of the current statistics. Writing for TechCrunch, Paul Carr presented several of the "no big deal" arguments. Unfortunately, he brings up the library as a place where books have always been free, saying that even though he is staunchly against large-scale pirating for personal gain, "when it comes to peer-to-peer file sharing, however, I'm calm to the point of apathy. The reason: books have *always* been free to those who don't want to pay for them. Since as far back as the seventeenth century, people too poor, or too cheap, to buy a book could walk into a public library and borrow it. In most civilized countries, a fund was established to pay authors a royalty on those loans—but the amount per author was so vanishingly small as to be meaningless" (P. Carr 2011).

While it's helpful that he distinguishes the library from large-scale pirate operations, this argument does not help to endear libraries to publishers or authors. It also ignores the difference between borrowing and torrenting. Libraries do ask that people bring materials back, for one, and have a long history of discouraging illegal behaviors. An older article from *PC World* makes the somewhat more compelling case that pirating of music was more common when people had Mp3 players but no legitimate way of buying digital music and that the built-in bookstores on eBook readers will keep most readers on the up-and-up when it comes to their eBooks (Keir 2010).

On FutureBook, Matteo Berlucchi points readers to a German organization, Libreka (Berlucchi 2012a), that uses watermarks to protect books rather than DRM and have found no instances of their watermarked books being pirated ("Social DRM and Epub"). Piracy and DRM are inextricably linked, frustrating anti-DRM advocates who are rarely propiracy. Piracy is central to almost any discussion about access to eBooks, and preventing piracy is a huge concern to publishers, distributors, booksellers, and librarians alike. Tellingly, a Google search for "eBooks privacy" asks if the searcher meant "eBooks piracy."

Most of the proposed solutions to piracy start with the same premise: nothing will end piracy entirely. Writing for Forbes, Paul Tassi observes that "as technology continues to evolve, the battle between pirates and copyright holders is going to escalate, and pirates are always, always going to be one step ahead. But what's clear is that legislation is not the answer. Piracy is already illegal in the US, and most places around the world, yet it persists underground, but more often in plain sight. Short of passing a law that allows the actual blacklisting of websites like China and Iran, there is no legislative solution" (Tassi 2012). Tassi suggests that instead, we recognize piracy as a "service problem" because (in the case of his article, he's talking about movies) studios have made downloading legal copies of movies difficult or impossible, and very expensive, while piracy is easy. He chastises the studios for their inability to assess the marketplace, criticizing the common practice of bundling a $30 Blu-ray with the "Ultraviolet" copy for selected digital devices. "Please, how about I'll give you $10 for the new Harry Potter, and I'll watch it whenever and wherever I want? This is a negotiation where at any time, your customer could just go download the damn movie for free, and they're doing *you* a favor by even *considering* picking it up legally. And you have the nerve to think it's on YOUR terms? That's not how negotiation works. It may not be right, but it's reality, and they have to face it" (Tassi 2012).

Making content (be it movies, books, or music) easy to obtain (and use legally) will attract large numbers of buyers, as iTunes has shown. The "there will always be pirates" argument is perhaps less compelling for those who make their living by selling content, but Berlucchi's exhortation to prosecute pirates without penalizing average buyers may have more traction. Cory Doctorow offers some longer-range perspective, observing that transitions in how we access information and entertainment have always been difficult. "Vaudeville performers had to transition to radio, an abrupt shift from having perfect control over who could hear a performance (if they don't buy a ticket, you throw them out) to no control whatsoever (any family whose 12-year-old could build a crystal set, the day's equivalent of installing file-sharing software, could tune in). There were business models for radio, but predicting them a priori wasn't easy" (Doctorow 2008, 76). However, Doctorow also offers publishers a much harder task for the future, piracy or no: a wholesale reinvention of their business models. "I don't think it's practical to charge for copies of electronic works. Bits aren't ever going to get harder to copy. So we'll have to figure out how to charge for something else" (Doctorow 2008, 76). His publisher, Tor, was happy to let him give away books online, though, and found that giving away eBooks helped to sell his printed books. That was in 2006, though, in a pre-Kindle, pre-iPad economy. However, Doctorow continues to give away eBooks (I happily downloaded *Content* from his site and put it on my Nook), and his books continue to sell. His model may not work for every author, but it makes piracy of his work impossible and has yet to damage his career.

INTERLIBRARY LOAN

ILL may be one of the unsung heroes in librarianship, a field brimming with the underacknowledged. It connects the patrons of the tiniest, most isolated library to the resources of the world. ILL is what allows librarians to offer access to any information a patron might want. ILL is expensive, but at the core of the library is access to information, regardless of how inconveniently located that information may be.

However, ILL is paper based. We might scan an article and eMail a PDF, but licensing agreements generally prevent us from sharing articles from databases ("Copyright in the Library"). eBooks are locked down even further, making it impossible for libraries to share eBooks as we have shared paper books. Within consortia, an eBook collection might be centrally purchased and access shared, but patrons cannot access the collections of a neighboring consortium.

Without the ability to share our collections, libraries become walled gardens. It's not likely that a library will purchase a rare orchid for one patron. If that patron can't make the trek to the library that specializes in orchids, she will simply go without. Right now, most libraries are buying widely available content electronically, and digitization is improving access to local history and other unique collections. But the inability to share eBooks flies in the face of the mission of libraries. Depending on how the future of eBooks unfolds, unshareable eBooks could simply mean a shift in how libraries approach collection development, or they could rock the foundation of our organizations.

ILL is an expensive undertaking for any library, and it is frequently cheaper to simply buy the requested book. However, libraries may have more flexibility in spending on staff time and less in a materials budget, making ILL the best or even only way to provide a patron with a requested item. Sometimes, ILL is the only answer, particularly in academic libraries where it may not be cheaper or even possible to buy the requested item. In public libraries, book groups pose a challenge, especially for smaller libraries. A library in a town of 5,000 people does not need to own 12 copies of *Water for Elephants*, but ILL can keep a book group in trade paperbacks for years.

Making decisions about eBooks based largely on the ability to ILL those eBooks is perhaps too much the tail wagging the dog. The loss of ILL in the eBook environment becomes increasingly problematic as more of our collections are purchased and managed through vendors and ruled by licensing agreements. If rental options were available for single-use items, that might take the place of ILL in practical terms, but it neuters the spirit of resource sharing and library collaboration.

CHAPTER 6

Libraries

PUBLIC LIBRARIES

Public libraries have been at the heart of the recent eBook explosion. Academic libraries have been using eBooks since 1999, and many public libraries began with eAudiobooks and some eBooks shortly after that. However, the introduction of the Kindle in 2007 vaulted eBooks into mainstream consciousness and brought the issue to the front desk of every public library in the country. Librarians have found themselves rushing to keep up with the early adopters, and educating patrons who are eBook reticent.

Unfortunately, this often means that libraries are caught between patron expectations, vendor restrictions, and publishers' demands. Patrons don't understand why they have to wait for an eBook ("it's just a file") or why libraries can't offer certain titles. For the most part, libraries are using vendor-provided platforms, leaving staff unable to address usability concerns or patron complaints about the interface.

Because OverDrive has been the dominant vendor for so long, it's not uncommon for librarians to voice concerns that OverDrive is not representing or advocating for libraries and library interests to publishers. As 3M and EBSCO expand their presence in the public library marketplace, it will be interesting to see how they handle things like publishers removing their eBooks from library collections. For public libraries, the hesitance of most of the Big Six publishers to work with libraries has been troubling. There are, of course, wonderful books from independent publishers and small presses that patrons are eager to read. However, it is hard to explain that we are unable to fulfill a request for a bestseller because it comes from a major publisher that doesn't sell eBooks for the library market. This is the first time in recent memory that libraries have been in the position of forcing patrons to care about which publisher their desired volume comes from. Publisher is not how most people think about their reading material.

For public library patrons, availability is paramount. While eBooks have been present in libraries since 1999, public libraries did not see intense interest in them until eReaders became more commonplace. In many ways, they have followed the path of eAudiobooks, which were initially available for most Mp3 players, but not iPods—once eAudiobooks were available for iPods, interest increased. Overdrive has only recently been able to make eBooks available for the Kindle, which has increased demand, but made publishers even more leery of library lending. 3M has said they are also pursuing Kindle compatibility. As with eAudiobooks, people may ask if the library has eBooks, but what they mean is "do you have books for my particular device?" If the library cannot provide eBooks for a patron's device, that patron may simply revert to print (which is likely not his or her preferred way to read) (Phaxia and Parsons 2011) or choose to buy or pirate the book instead. Or possibly not read the book at all. Anecdotally, this is not an uncommon reaction from devoted eBook readers—if a book can't be found at the library or under a certain price point, some readers simply opt not to read the book.

eReaders are inherently personal devices. They're designed for a single user, and that user's credit card. Public libraries have experimented with loaning out eReaders, either already loaded with titles or by buying a title for each patron who borrows the device. There have been questions about the legality of these programs, with individual librarians being told by Amazon that loaning Kindles is acceptable, but an Amazon spokesperson telling *Library Journal* that it is not (Porter, Weaver, and Newman 2012, 124). Loaning eReaders is a way to offer patrons a "try it before you buy it" experience with an eReader; so rather than tangle with legal questions, many libraries buy the devices for staff to learn on and use and to offer eReader petting zoos to the public, and eReader help sessions for patrons who own their own devices. At the Douglas County Library System in Colorado, staff are given small stipends to offset the cost of a personal purchase of a device. The library maintains a large list of qualifying devices, and while the stipend is not enough to cover the entire cost of an eReader, the program highlights the personal nature of the device (Sendze 2012). While a shared staff stash of gadgets helps everyone in the library gain familiarity with eBook troubleshooting, owning and regularly using an eReader breeds a facility that a week-long stint of eReading cannot.

Offering eBooks is not an insignificant undertaking for any library. For a public library with a diminishing budget, finding the money to buy a product like OverDrive, never mind a few eReaders for staff to learn on, can be daunting, if not impossible. Because eBooks are a hot topic right now, some

Friends groups are happy to fund eBooks, and many consortia offer access to eBooks for members and nonmembers. Keeping up with demand can be time consuming. eBooks typically have long wait lists, even with a limited number of publishers' content available. Speaking to *Library Journal*, eBook buyers shared tips on how to keep an OverDrive collection fresh. Christopher Platt, director of collections and circulation operations at New York Public Library emphasized the need to focus on content and Jen Wright, assistant chief of the Materials Management Division at the Free Library of Philadelphia told LJ that she made frequent purchases from OverDrive rather than placing larger orders less often (Orr 2011). *Library Journal* also found that "libraries are all over the map when it comes to budget" (Orr 2011), with each library carving out a percentage of their materials budget they could afford, while still trying to meet demand.

As the public library eBook marketplace gets more competitive, and companies start rolling out more sophisticated services like OverDrive's Want It Now platform, libraries will have to continue to find their footing. eBooks can easily eat up a huge portion of a materials budget, which leaves the digital have-nots in the cold. But the allure of adding an eBook platform is hard to resist. It all but guarantees local media coverage and positive attention from at least some town residents. I've had a few Google alerts set up for eBook news and library news, and every day there are stories in local papers about libraries offering eBook services. The danger, of course, is that as the demand for eBooks grows, the prices can climb beyond the reach of many libraries. Random House, arguably the most library-friendly of the Big Six, recently announced that they would sell eBooks to libraries unfettered by circulation restrictions but at a slightly higher price. The structure seems very much like library binding pricing, and it's certainly better for libraries than circulation restrictions or windowing practices (Albanese 2012b). However, right now the price is still somewhat tied to a print book. If a library eBook costs a little bit more, that increase is relative to the cost of a printed book. What academic libraries found with journals was that the relationship between print and electronic faded, and electronic prices soon skyrocketed past the point of affordability. Public libraries can ill-afford a similar fate.

ACADEMIC LIBRARIES

Academic libraries have been buying eBooks since 1999, when libraries began using NetLibrary products in addition to the offerings on Project Gutenberg. In 2010, academic libraries added 32,033,008 eBooks and 27,163,548 print volumes (books, serial backfiles, and government documents) (Phan et al. 2011). eBook purchasing at academic libraries now runs the gamut from third-party vendors like EBL, ebrary, and Gale to individual publishers like Springer and Elsevier. Academic libraries may buy individual titles or bulk packages of titles in particular subject areas, and they have been spearheading patron-driven acquisition (PDA) (Schell 2011, 78–79). Scholars and students have very different needs than those reading for pleasure, so academic models for eBook access and use are often very different from those in public libraries. Academic publishers are often more willing to extend simultaneous use and innovative combinations of print and electronic formats are beginning to emerge. *Publishers Weekly* reported Oxford University Press is working with Manhattan Research Library Initiative and Triangle Research Libraries Network to offer eBooks and affordable print copies that can be shared between institutions (Albanese 2012d).

PDA allows patrons to see a broad catalog of titles and obtain access to those that the library has not purchased. Plans vary, of course, but generally speaking, PDA charges the library when patrons have accessed a book. Libraries can buy varying levels of access or simply buy any book a patron requests, unless it exceeds a cost threshold agreed upon by the library and the vendor. For academic libraries, this represents a transition from a "just in case" collection to a "just in time" one (Murray 2006). While one of the fears voiced by librarians has been that PDA undermines the value of collection development, the ability to let faculty and students access material they need without requiring the library to purchase it or wait for ILL could serve to keep the collection focused by separating collection development from the temporary interest of a patron.

Writing at *The Scholarly Kitchen*, Rick Anderson suggests that the tension between PDA and collection development specialists can be resolved by defining the "A" of PDA more carefully: "The bottom line, I think, is that each library needs to decide what problem it's trying to solve with PDA . . . if you want to build a better collection, then you probably want to do patron-driven *acquisition*, and PDA is likely going to play a relatively peripheral role in your collection-building strategies. If you want to make the collection itself less of an issue, and instead focus on giving your researchers dynamic and real-time access to relevant and useful content, then your focus should be on patron-driven *access* . . . These aren't mutually exclusive strategies, but it does matter where you focus your money and energy" (Espositio 2012).

Not all librarians are convinced, however. In 2010, on Inside Higher Ed, Barbara Fister voiced concerns about the usefulness of PDA for undergraduates. She cited a study by Project Information Literacy (Head and Eisenberg 2010), saying it "clarifies something I've long sensed: undergraduates don't necessarily need a bigger banquet. They need a limited number of good choices, not all-you-can-eat" (Fister 2010). Fister also observes that for undergraduates (and I think we can extrapolate to younger students as well), there are times when a print book is preferable for research. She cites primary-source content from the Middle Ages, saying, "Yes, you can search the full text, but novices have a difficult time knowing what words might yield results. Trying to guess what words used in a 12th century text is even trickier. The kind of browsing that works for them—flipping pages, sampling contents, comparing texts side-by-side—seems to be simply easier with printed texts" (Fister 2010).

Fister has also called for academic libraries to share their electronic journal costs as part of the open-access movement in scholarly communications. She and other academic librarians began speaking out about the price hikes coming from large publishers on content colleges and universities often need to have. She assures her readers that "I'm not just being snarky; I know this kind of high-quality publishing costs money. Fine. I know that faculty are producing more research and presumably somebody's got to publish it. But the only way I can afford to keep these journals (and I can't afford not to) is to cut other things. Smaller societies, university presses? Sorry—you'll be getting less of my money. I'll do this because I have to, but dammit—this is *so wrong*" (Fister 2011). Scholars have also been pushing back against academic publishers, with faculty at MIT (Duranceau 2012) and other institutions boycotting Elsevier for its support of the Research Works Act. While this is not directly eBook related, there is a shift in how academics perceive publishers, and indicates that library patrons may take an interest in the relationships between library, vendor, and publisher. Indeed, a compelling case can be made that the public library's path with eBooks will mirror the academic library's experience with journals, as Brett Bonfield explains in his post "The Ebook Cargo Cult" on In the Library with the Lead Pipe (Bonfield 2012).

Preservation

Academic libraries must also consider issues of preservation, which are much more complicated when content is digital. Preservation comes up for public libraries and private consumers—what happens to my Kindle books when I die? (As it turns out, unless Amazon intervenes and deletes content, Kindle books may live as long as your account does, so if you pass along your username and password, your heirs can use your Amazon.com account) (Jarrard 2012). But in an academic setting, the issue of preservation is complicated by archives, researchers looking for historical content and context, and collection development policies, and it is academic organizations that are tackling issues of preservation, notably through projects like HathiTrust.

Somewhere in your office or house, there is doubtless a box of disks. They may be 3.5" or 5.25" or you may (like me) have a stack of zip disks somewhere. Even if you can get the appropriate hardware to read those disks, you may not be able to access any of the files on them (I'm fairly certain my stack of zip disks includes documents written on MacWrite and Claris-Works). An eBook that can be accessed only through a vendor's platform presents much the same problem. Even if libraries were given all of their eBook files, who's to say that those file formats will even open in a few years? One of the original eBook standards, OEB, has already been replaced by ePub (Romano 2002). (Romano's report is worth looking at, just to see how much things have changed in the last several years. eBooks aren't as new as we sometimes think they are and the current players haven't always been so powerful. One thing hasn't changed: librarians issuing a call to arms to their colleagues.) Strategies like emulation and migration are possible, but require us to plan now for the future. Emulation, which you may be familiar with if you've ever played older computer or video games online, "[requires] a deep understanding of existing hardware and software" (Kirchhoff 2012, 76), while migrating files forward into new formats "requires a deep understanding of the content being preserved" (Kirchhoff 2012, 76). Other data must also be taken into consideration, like metadata and provenance.

Portico is digital preservation service from ITHAKA, a nonprofit organization dedicated to digital preservation for the academic community. ITHAKA is also the parent organization to JSTOR. Portico's website defines digital preservation as including usability, authenticity, discoverability, and accessibility and not as backup, system redundancy, or replication. Organizations like Portico work with both libraries and publishers to preserve digital content, a strategy that acknowledges the complexities of copyright in digital preservation. Digital preservation can violate an author's copyright. "Migration, for example, may be a violation of the copyright owner's right to prepare a derivative work. Making a digital work broadly available may impinge on the copyright owner's distribution, performance, and display rights. Preserving a password-protected or encrypted file may require violating the copyright owner's exclusive right to control access" ("Legal Issues").

Preservation is also complicated by the changeable nature of eBooks. Retractions, editions, and any updates to content are rendered fluid in an eBook environment. A preservation strategy must include decisions about how to handle these changes to text. Unlike with physical objects, preservation is often outsourced, leaving the library to wonder what will happen if a preservation agency goes out of business. Organizations like CLOCKSS, a multinational nonprofit venture of publishers and research libraries, bank on the community to keep the digital archive safe ("FAQ" CLOCKSS).

Digital preservation is still in its infancy. eBook collections create enormous complications for preservationists, far beyond the already complicated issues of digitization. DRM, copyright, hardware, and file format conspire to make librarians wonder if future generations will be able to read the content we have today. Current file format standards are not designed to be archival (Carpenter 2012). Preservation is tied up with ownership and access. As large academic institutions tackle the question, public librarians and private citizens are looking at their eBook collections and devices and wondering what will happen to it all if OverDrive or Amazon folds or the cost of the platform gets too high.

SCHOOL LIBRARIES

"Don't buy eBooks" was Christopher Harris's rallying cry at the *Library Journal/School Library Journal* Ebook Summit in 2011. eBooks, Harris says, make economic sense only when they're purchased by consortia. School libraries face their unique pressures, from national standards, to curriculum requirements, to specific circulation patterns. For example, most states have adopted the Common Core State Standards, which "stipulates that at least half of reading assignments be literary nonfiction for all grades. These are works written in a narrative style, which can be supplemented by primary source documents such as letters and journals. In addition, the Common Core recommends using excerpts of text to directly address a learning objective related to science or social studies standards" (Harris 2011). School libraries must build collections that support these standards, with content appropriate for each grade level that fits into the curriculum developed by their schools.

Harris points out that while public libraries are struggling to find a way forward with publishers and resellers of popular titles, school-oriented publishers are likely to offer simultaneous access to eBooks, recognizing that many titles are likely to be needed by an entire grade at the same time. He offers an example of a K–5 school with 600 students, where the fourth grade is four classes of 25 students each. A book about a topic the fourth grade is studying is going to be read by only 100 students, so "unlimited, simultaneous access becomes nothing more than a marketing term—not a projection of actual usage. This is why a library consortia model is the way to go" (Harris 2011). Extrapolating from that example, Harris says that "the same formula extends to larger groups. Many K–12 publishers recognize that providing an ebook beyond a single school to a group of 50 schools doesn't necessarily mean 50 times the use. Therefore many publishers offer price breaks to consortia purchasing ebooks" (Harris 2011).

Harris goes on to advocate for eBook purchases made by consortia of schools pooling their current funds to create large collections. K–12 publishers and resellers offer platforms that allow for simultaneous use, though at least one reseller, Follett, says that licensing agreements with publishers prohibit simultaneous-use eBooks to be shared by multiple buildings ("eBook FAQ" FollettShelf).

School Library Journal's 2011 Technology Survey found that while eBooks account for only 0.5 percent of school library collections, school librarians predict that number will rise to 7.8 percent by 2016 ("SLJ's 2011 Technology Survey: Things Are Changing Fast"). That future will likely be unevenly distributed, with some schools embracing eBooks (like Cushing Academy, which in 2009 famously moved to an all-electronic library) and others lacking the funding or technology to go digital. Consortial buying is a way to lower the cost for everyone and allow underfunded schools to try eBooks at a lower cost.

Some school libraries are experimenting with eReaders, like Buffy Hamilton's Kindle and Nook programs at the Unquiet Library in Canton, Georgia. Hamilton purchased Kindles for her library and loaned them to students during the 2010–11 school year, a program that was very successful at her school and that Hamilton documented well on her blog. In July 2011, she posted on her blog that she would not be buying any more Kindles for her school, as the end user license agreement (EULA) had changed and now required a separate Amazon account for each Kindle the library owns without (at the time) offering a back-end tool to help library staff manage the library's Kindle content (Hamilton 2011b).

Hamilton moved to Nook Simple Touches in the 2011–12 school year to support classroom novel studies and literature circle studies at her school. Barnes & Noble offers a back-end solution for educational institutions called B&N Managed Program. Hamilton characterizes it as "[though[not a *perfect* solution nor one that allows schools to deliver ebook content to student owned devices or across multiple platforms, this is a more viable solution for the needs of the K12 environment in terms of options that meet our purchasing needs and ability to manage the content effectively and efficiently while giving us a means to offer students a digital reading experience that we hope will engage readers of all ages and prior reading experiences" (Hamilton 2011a).

Other school libraries are hoping to emulate Douglas County in Colorado and offer textbooks and other eBooks on a server hosted in-house (Goerner 2012). In addition to offering eBooks, this would allow the school library to publish student and faculty work in eBook form. Writing for the Digital Shift, school media specialist Phil Goerner observed, "Libraries have the opportunity to support aspiring writers by assisting in their research, connecting them with local authors, and introducing them to established editors or professionals involved in publicity and marketing. This is the stuff we're already good at and now we'll be able to publish and stream their work online" (Goerner 2012).

In addition to the technical challenges faced in the K–12 environment, school libraries are bound by curriculum standards, state laws, and student and faculty needs. Faculty and administration may be eBook boosters or critics. Parents may not support eBook use in the schools. Anecdotal evidence about kids and eBooks is mixed. Early in 2011, the *New York Times* reported that eBook sales of young adult and children's literature was up, and profiled several preteens and teenagers who began reading more once they had eReaders (Bosman 2011). More recently, the *Times'* parenting blog featured a study done at Temple University that found that parents interact differently with their children over an eReader than a print book and that children absorbed more of the story and understood it better when parents used a print book (Dell'Antonia 2011). Reporting about younger children and their parents shows a discomfort with eBooks for small children, but is often focused on learning to read and leisure reading, not homework (Hsu 2011, Richtel and Bosman 2011).

For many school libraries, eBooks are a school- or district-wide undertaking. A superintendent might want to pilot a tablet program or create high-tech classrooms. A move to eTextbooks requires even larger collaboration and funding. Tech blog Gizmodo, while enthusiastic about Apple's iBooks for the classroom, points out that "while iBooks are very affordable textbooks, the iPad makes for one insanely expensive backpack" (Barrett 2012). Not only are the iPads themselves pricey (and not ready to be a laptop replacement for a paper-writing student), but the books will add up over the long term, says Gizmodo's Brian Barrett. While the textbooks in iBooks are inexpensive, "the business model in this place is clear: instead of selling an updated textbook every 5–10 years for $100, update and sell every year for $15. And it'll work; it's not like you can hand down an iBook from year to year. In fact, you expressly can't" (Barrett 2012). Additionally, as Sarah Ludwig, Library Department chair at Hamden Hall, observed, a school could build a curriculum around an electronic textbook, only to have the publisher or vendor change their ability to access that eBook. Author David Sirota fears that technology-laden classrooms are simply "the allure of a quick fix, as gadgets seem to hold out the possibility that school districts can sustain huge budget cuts without sacrificing quality tutelage. The idea is that teachers can be replaced by cheaper computers, at once saving schools money, preventing tax increases for school resources, and preserving educational services. Even if data prove that's a pipe dream, the desire for a cure-all has convinced many desperate schools to chase the fantasy" (Sirota 2012).

The worry that investing in the cutting-edge technology of iBooks is harmful to schools is also expressed by Barrett at Gizmodo: "What all this adds up to is an education revolution for the landed gentry. Or even worse, schools that can't afford it chasing a wave that's years away from cresting. Millions of dollars spent on a supplementary learning tool. A distant horizon mistaken for the here and now" (Barrett 2012). In their chapter in *No Shelf Required 2*, Jennifer LaGarde and Christine James encourage school librarians to make sure that an eReader program supports instructional goals, saying that as Myrtle Grove Middle School embarked on a Nook initiative, "it was vital that the e-readers be more than just a gimmick to grab students' attention. Nooks being a new electronic device would keep students focused only for a short time and wouldn't guarantee that learning ensued. It was clear that without intentional planning and solid content, the Nooks would quickly lose credibility, as would the media specialist and teachers who had pushed for their purchase" (LaGarde and James 2012, 194).

The advantages to electronic content loom large for school librarians, and publishers and vendors are working to meet the needs of schools, says Christopher Harris. Specifically, he says that there are a large number of nonfiction titles for K–12 readers available in different formats and under a number of licensing agreements, including unlimited, simultaneous access. Additionally, publishers are enhancing eBooks to meet the new Common Core State Standards, "for example, enhanced social studies ebooks from Rosen Publishing include maps, timelines, and primary-source documents. Larger publishers of reference works are also working with school libraries to meet their specialized needs for district access to a common set of resources. Many publishers and vendors in the school library sector are working with districts and library systems to provide consortia-access pricing" (Harris 2012). Schools can also benefit from accessibility measures, like the U.S. Department of Education's Bookshare.org, which supplies free DAISY eBooks with enhancements designed to help students with disabilities. Also, there is some evidence that eReaders can help struggling or reluctant readers (Harris 2012).

School Library Journal covered the story of Julie Hume, a school media specialist who conducted her own experiment with Tumblebooks and reluctant readers. Hume took two groups of struggling readers and tested them before any interventions to get a baseline, then she gave one group Tumblebooks and the other received the reading interventions the school had used in the past. She found that the students using Tumblebooks surpassed the results of their print-based peers. Three months into the project, "the average fluency rate for the Tumblebook group was 23 percentage points higher than that of the control group. Students using the ebooks had moved from a Lexile level of K to M. By January, the entire group of children in the ebook program had achieved fluency to the point that they were 'exited' from her pull-out sessions and integrated back into their regular classrooms. It took the control group two months longer" (Guernsey 2011). Similar results were found by school librarian Kathy Parker and a group of teachers in Seneca Grade School District 170 in Illinois. In *No Shelf Required 2*, she details the Kindle 2 pilot program launched in 2009. The school purchased 18 new Kindle 2s to be used by a group of reluctant readers and a group of advanced readers. What they found was that the ability to manipulate the text was a boon to both groups. For the reluctant readers, the ability to look up words and highlight passages proved particularly useful in increasing reading comprehension (Parker 2012, 216). The inability to see how long a book is also encouraged students to try reading books that may have intimidated in print (Parker 2012, 217).

These small experiments tantalize, but do not yet provide large-scale data. While pleased with the results of her program, Hume told *School Library Journal* that " 'I think Tumblebooks should be for intervention only,' ... For confidence-building and self-esteem, she explains, the electronic book is unparalleled. But at some point, she says, you have to stop 'the handholding' " (Guernsey 2011).

CHAPTER 7

The Readers

ADULTS

Adults are usually the default when we're talking about eBooks. Children and teens are seen as separate groups, with their own interests and needs. For publishers, it's adults who buy books and eBooks, and adults are the primary consumers of eBooks. As with any relatively new technology, there are concerns about the effect on our brains, society, and how we interact with each other and the written word. Essayists lament the end of the casual nosiness afforded by book covers on subways or on coffee tables. The popularity of eBooks gets the credit and blame for a myriad of social trends and even the success of specific titles. Articles about the 2012 phenomenon of *50 Shades of Grey* often chalked up at least some of the popularity of the books to eReaders, which allowed embarrassed readers to enjoy the erotic novels privately. However, romance and erotica have been popular genres long before the eReader came on the book scene.

eBooks have had the most success so far as predominantly text files. Books that require extensive illustration or specific layouts, such as children's books or cookbooks, have been less popular in eBook format. Additionally, the "gift economy" around both children's and cookbooks was mentioned repeatedly at both Digital Book World 2012 and Tools of Change 2012. At Digital Book World, a panel on the new ePub3 standard discussed the increasing ability to incorporate interactive features like calculators in nutrition books that might have contained tables in print. However, the move to eBooks was led by heavy readers buying text-based books. Bowker's and BISG's data indicate that eBook adoption has moved beyond the early-adopter phase (Schechner 2012) and has become more popular with even casual readers and gadget buyers ("EBook Consumers Say 'Yes' to Tablets, Says BISG Study").

Unlike the expected-adoption curve, eBooks are more popular with slightly older adults. Bowker's UK office found that among British adults, eBook sales were driven largely by adults aged 45 to 54. Younger adults were heavy buyers of eBooks, but their consumption was leveling off, while those over 45 continued to increase their eBook purchases (Baddeley 2012). This is not surprising, given the advantages eBooks offer to anyone who prefers larger print (but not the inconveniences of large-print books), as well as baby boomers' love of both reading and gadgets. Pew's Internet & American Life project found that while younger adults were more likely to have read a book in part or in whole in the last year (though, to be fair, this includes people 16 and up, who may have been reading for schoolwork), it was older adults who read the most. Adults 65 and up read on average 23 books a year, while younger adults numbers hovered in the teens. When it comes to eBooks, Pew found that those most likely to have read an eBook in the last year were 18 to 39, but noted that "Those who own tablets and e-readers who are over 40 years old are more likely than those under 40 to read daily on their digital devices" (Rainie 2012b).

Resistance to eBooks among adults also exists. Both Verso's and Pew Internet & American Life's research found that among those who do not have eReaders, a percentage are not planning on buying them. Verso's research found that resistance was actually increasing. They estimate that resistance among the book-reading population will level out at around 50 percent (Verso Digital). Pew found that the most common reason given was "Just don't need one/don't want one" (Rainie 2012b), which accounted for 24 percent of those who were not interested in eReaders and 35 percent of those resistant to tablets. The cost of the device was the second most popular reason given, with 19 percent saying it was the reason they didn't plan to buy an eReader and 25 percent saying it was stopping them from getting a tablet (Rainie 2012b). Resistance could be cost related or philosophical; both kinds of objections are likely to diminish over time, as devices get cheaper, technology evolves, and eReaders and tablets become more common. Librarians likely talk to a large number of people who are resistant to eReading, and it can seem like there are plenty of people who will never make the leap. I have friends and colleagues who say the idea of looking at a screen for leisure after looking at one for work all day doesn't appeal. I completely understand, but wonder if they'll be carrying around iPads with E Ink switches in a couple of years. I also wonder what we'll see in adult eReading habits as those growing up and coming of age with eBooks now become adults.

CHILDREN'S LIT AND LITERACY

Children and eBooks

Children and eBooks get a lot of media attention. Schools that hand out iPads to students are alternately pilloried and celebrated. Technology is either making us smarter and more productive than we've ever been before or ruining our brains. Critics like Nicholas Carr contend that the Internet has changed how we seek out, consume, and process information for the worse. Enthusiasts counter that technology can improve our minds and that almost anything we do requires our brains to make some sort of trade-off. Literacy itself caused the ancient Greeks some angst about lost skills (Agger 2010).

eBooks are no exception to the love/hate relationship we have with kids and technology. eReading technology is either making it easier for kids to learn to read or destroying any chance of having a literate population in 20 years. I'm being flip, but eBooks and kids has proven to be a polarizing topic. Popular news stories cite parental discomfort with the ritual bedtime story read from a glowing screen. Parents observe that the built-in narration in some children's eBooks goes too quickly and has to be paused to field questions (Hsu 2011). Particularly popular these days are stories about the children of high-tech workers who eschew eBooks for their little ones (Richtel and Bosman 2011) or even screens in their kids' educational environment (Richtel 2011).

Right now, most of what we have are anecdotes and theory about kids and eBooks. The NEA has found that the number of books in a child's home is correlated with academic success (independent of the parents' education) (NEA 2007, 71). Since 2007 (the year the report was published) eBooks have exploded, and while the NEA says "access to printed matter is associated positively with test scores for a variety of subjects" (NEA 2007, 71), we don't know if that would also be true in a home with fewer print books, but a large number of eBooks.

Pew's Internet & American Life Project found that when it comes to reading to children, people prefer print by a very large margin. Among respondents, 81 percent said that print was better for reading with a child, as opposed to 9 percent who preferred eBooks (Rainie 2012b). This fits in with the anecdotes reported in the media, citing parental preference for print. Studies on children and technology are only just beginning to include eBooks and eReading. A 40-year retrospective study on children and technology found that "in those classrooms where computers were used to support teaching, the technology was found to have a small to moderate positive impact on both learning and attitude" (EurekaAlert 2012) and that technology works best when "students are encouraged to think critically and communicate effectively" (EurekaAlert 2012).

As Sesame Street publishing executive Jennifer Perry told Publishing Perspectives, " 'The problem is that digital publishing is so new, that very little work has been done on how kids interface with new technology,' she says. 'When we decided to convert our bestselling book ever ([*The*] *Monster* [*at the End of This Book*]), we looked for research on devices. How do preschoolers interact with e-books? How will their experience with the content change from the printed page? We found nothing' " (Kalder 2011). Like many other publishers, Sesame Street is developing eBooks and apps for children. However, they are also conducting research into the questions Perry poses.

Hopefully, Sesame Street's studies will be just the beginning; "in addition to research conducted by an educational, nonprofit organization like Sesame Street, the children's book publishing industry could benefit from independent, academic research on the topic" (Greenfield 2011a). Until we have more data, it will be difficult to tell how iPad story times are impacting young children. Regardless of what those studies discover, librarians will be working with tech-savvy children every day. School-age kids use PowerPoint, make videos, and create blogs for assignments and often spend their free time online as well.

Transliteracy

Advocates of transliteracy believe that literacy has expanded beyond reading and writing and beyond what librarians usually call information literacy to encompass consuming and creating across multiple platforms. Professor Alan Liu, director of the Transcriptions Research Project, a project of the Department of English at the University of California at Santa Barbara, developed the Transliteracies Project in 2005. The first Transliteracies conference took place that year, and inspired Sue Thomas, a faculty member at De Montfort University in Leicester, UK, to return home and begin work on transliteracy. In 2006, the Production and Research in Transliteracy (PART) group was formed (Thomas et al. 2007). In a 2007 paper, PART researchers discuss the difficulty in defining transliteracy as opposed to media literacy. The group found that "our current thinking (although still not entirely resolved) is that because it offers a wider analysis of reading, writing and interacting across a range of platforms, tools, media and cultures, transliteracy does not replace, but rather contains, 'media literacy' and also 'digital literacy' " (Thomas et al. 2007). They note, however, that "transliteracy is not just about computer–based materials, but about all communication types across time and culture. It does not privilege one above the other but treats all as of equal value and moves between and across them" (Thomas et al. 2007).

In libraries, that debate continues today. The Libraries and Transliteracy blog has hosted a number of lively discussions on the meaning and value of transliteracy. Children's eBooks and hybrid books (books that may be read in paper form but that also contain an online or social component) are prime examples of transliterate work—the convergence of text, video, social inter-action, and perhaps even content creation in one story. In 2008, the *New York Times* profiled several teenagers who did much or most of their reading online, noting that "clearly, reading in print and on the Internet are differ-ent. On paper, text has a predetermined beginning, middle and end, where readers focus for a sustained period on one author's vision. On the Internet, readers skate through cyberspace at will and, in effect, compose their own beginnings, middles and ends" (Rich 2008). The article notes that despite concern from adults that children aren't getting the same benefits by reading online that they would get from reading a book, "young people 'aren't as troubled as some of us older folks are by reading that doesn't go in a line,' said Rand J. Spiro, a professor of educational psychology at Michigan State University who is studying reading practices on the Internet. 'That's a good thing because the world doesn't go in a line, and the world isn't organized into separate compartments or chapters' " (Rich 2008).

Transmedia titles are not limited to eBooks and apps. The 39 Clues series, which "[combines] books, collectable game cards, and an interactive website" (Fleishhacker 2011) to engage kids with the story, was an early example of cross-platform content for children. Enhanced eBooks are a hot topic in eBooks right now, and they bring some of these transmedia issues to the fore. But many worry that the current crop of enhanced eBooks is nothing more than vaguely literary games and movies.

Enhanced eBooks

Salon's Laura Miller identifies a fundamental problem for many readers who do not find enhanced eBooks to be as engrossing as text. Adding video and other interactive features "keep[s] bumping up against this fundamental problem: You can't really pay much attention to anything else while you're reading, so in order to play with any of these new features, you have to *stop* reading. If you're enjoying what you're reading, then the attentional tug of all these peripheral doodads is vaguely annoying, and if you're not engaged by the story, they aren't enough on their own to win you over" (L. Miller 2012). She focuses on children's books, pointing out that enhanced eBooks are often children's books because they have always included illustrations and images. These books, she says, are often light on the story and, though lovely, not designed to promote literacy in children. Miller says that when it comes to enhanced eBooks that "marginalize" text, "while the result is charm-ing, no parents should kid themselves that it will help teach their kids to read; it's more likely to teach them how to play 'Angry Birds' " (L. Miller 2012).

A small study backs Miller's observations. The Joan Ganz Cooney Center at Sesame Workshop found that children aged three to six preferred reading eBooks to print books and their comprehension was the same, regardless of format. However, when enhanced eBooks were compared, "kids were more focused on tapping things and that took away from their comprehension as well as the interaction between the parent and the child" (Greenfield 2012), said senior consultant for industry studies at the Center, Carly Shuler. More study is clearly needed, though the plethora of apps and types of enhancements, platforms, and devices complicates any study (Greenfield 2012).

Many companies are focused on the benefits of eBooks for children. Jeremy Greenfield of Digital Book World spoke with a Hillel Cooperman, cofounder of A Story Before Bed, a start-up that allows parents to record themselves reading an eBook for their child. Cooperman's stance is that "what's great about children's books is that unlike any other book they were meant to be read together ... The question as whether you should read to your kids on a different medium is a stupid question. Reading to your kids is good, period" (Greenfield 2012).

Greenfield found that many others concurred with Cooperman, adding that "his sentiment was echoed by nearly every expert, observer and researcher we spoke with for this piece: It's good to read to your children, regardless of format ... At Sesame and Scholastic, part of the mission is to encourage reading, and devices that get kids excited about books are welcome, regardless if they're paper and binding or full-color touch-screen" (Greenfield 2012).

As more studies are done, we will have a more definitive understanding of how eBooks impact literacy and learning. Until then, parental and educational philosophy will dictate children's exposure to eBooks. This, of course, assumes that those children have access to eBooks. Greenfield also interviewed Carol Rasco, president and CEO of Reading Is Fundamental. She expressed fear of a new digital divide, saying "I fear that many of our children in low-income areas aren't going to have as much access to the readers themselves or tools needed to read the digital books. It's something that is really moving along and we're going to leave some of those children behind. They won't have the skills needed when schools, all of a sudden, go to e-readers for their text-books, perhaps" (Greenfield 2012).

DIGITAL DIVIDE

Libraries have been champions of bridging the digital divide since they started offering Internet access. In her excellent book, *Without A Net: Librarians Bridging the Digital Divide*, Jessamyn West says that "the digital divide is a simplistic phrase used to explain the gap between people who can easily use and access technology and those who cannot" (West 2011d, xxiv). She goes on to point out that when we see that things like computer ownership or broadband access are on the rise, it's important to take note of whom they are on the rise for. Additionally, "the problem is more complicated than simply having computers available. People who can physically sit down in

There are about as many websites devoted to children, parenting, and education as there are children in the world. Your favorite children's librarian can doubtless recommend several excellent sites. These are a few of my favorites:

Libraries and Transliteracy: http://librariesandtransliteracy.wordpress.com/. Whether you think transliteracy is simply information literacy dressed up in newfangled terms or you think it's going to revolutionize libraries, the Libraries and Transliteracy site has interesting posts, links, and presentations to peruse.

The Brilliant Blog: http://anniemurphypaul.com/blog/. Journalist and author Annie Murphy Paul is working on a book about learning called *Brilliant: The New Science of Smart*. She regularly posts links to studies, articles, and insights into how we learn and how our brains adapt to new technologies.

Mind/Shift: http://blogs.kqed.org/mindshift/. PBS's fantastic site devoted to technology in education. Worth signing up for the weekly eMail update so you don't miss something of interest.

Apophenia: http://www.zephoria.org/thoughts/. Famed researcher Danah Boyd writes regularly about teens, youth culture, and technology.

I found the sections about children the most challenging to write because there's so much contradictory information out there, and anything that deals with children and learning is bound to evoke strong opinions. My best tactic has been to take everything with a grain of salt and remember that each generation thinks the next one is ruined by changes in culture and technology.

front of a computer still don't necessarily know how to use one" (West 2011d, xxv). This same issue can be applied to eBooks. eReader ownership does not always translate into avid eBook reader (indeed, 9% of eReader owners surveyed by Pew's Internet & American Life project didn't know what kind they had). Of those surveyed by Pew who did not plan on buying eReaders, 5 percent didn't know what an eReader was, 4 percent said they didn't want to have to learn to use one, and 2 percent said they were too old. When it came to tablet computers, 7 percent said they didn't want to learn how to use one, 2 percent said they didn't know what a tablet computer was, and 2 percent said they were too old (Rainie 2012b).

Outside of the library world, there seems to be little concern about the have-nots. Some of that can be attributed to misconceptions (even homeless people have cell phones now) or disinterest. But plenty of people believe that the digital divide will simply be eradicated. Mike Shatzkin offered a not uncommon take, saying that the government and large corporations will need everyone to be online, so pricing broadband out of reach will soon be like pricing garbage collection out of reach (Shatzkin 2011f). While that future sounds wonderful, it will ring hollow to many librarians. West details the problems public librarians face when even moderately tech-savvy patrons start using OverDrive. In her rural communities, patrons often took the library's participation in an OverDrive audiobook consortium as a reason to buy an Mp3 player (West 2011d, 7), only to find themselves involved in a "complicated hokey-pokey system" (West 2011d, 28) that requires patrons and librarians to figure out

- Digital files and digital rights management
- Downloading and installing software
- Selecting and using an Mp3 player
- Upgrading software on their computer
- Explaining the difference between how OverDrive files behave and how most digital files behave (West 2011d, 28)

That particular divide will be experienced only by patrons fortunate enough to be able to get their hands on the necessary technology. eBooks present libraries with the unenviable task of offering something not all of our patrons can access. eBooks are an inherently personal technology. A borrowed, shared eReader is not a stopgap measure the way an Internet terminal is. Right now, most libraries are buying eBooks that they're also buying in print, but library eBook vendors are starting to work with authors who publish only in eBook format. "Unlike books, which are one of the few media that do not require a secondary external device for playback, e-books put additional barriers between readers and knowledge" (Mims 2011).

Personal stories of the saving grace of books and libraries are legion. Author Zadie Smith wrote a powerful essay for the BBC on her childhood and the salvation she found at the local library, which stirred up a tremendous amount of controversy (Anstice 2011) and is available only on YouTube (http://www.youtube.com/watch?v=vP5PJsRDrkM; the transcripts were removed). In 2011, author Seanan McGuire wrote about her own childhood poverty and how the low cost of books made them accessible to her. Declaring herself to be a technophile who loves her computer and smartphone, who loves that eBooks exist, she wrote: "This doesn't change the part where, every time a discussion of ebooks turns, seemingly inevitably, to 'Print is dead, traditional publishing is dead, all smart authors should be bailing to the brave new electronic frontier,' what I hear, however unintentionally, is 'Poor people don't deserve to read' " (McGuire 2011).

In an article about Pew's eBook research for PBS's Mind/Shift, Jenny Shank asks, "Do ebooks contribute to the digital divide?" She quotes Samantha Becker, research project manager of the U.S. IMAPCT Study at the University of Washington's Information School, as saying that eBooks are not contributing to the digital divide now, but could if eBooks become the dominant form that books take. Becker takes the lower rates of reading and technology adoption as a symptom of poverty rather than a cause (though it seems to be something of a vicious circle). Tellingly, and perhaps terrifyingly, she points to libraries as a solution, saying that libraries have always had access to reading and technology as their missions and that eBook access is part of that (Shank 2012).

On the one hand, it's wonderful to see libraries getting positive attention in the media. However, I couldn't help but feel a bit of panic at the confidence Becker has in libraries to bridge the eBook gap. The eBook digital divide is only going to become more complicated and more difficult to contend with. Libraries are already struggling to keep up with consumers. If a patron who can't afford an eReader wants to use the library to borrow an enhanced eBook from a publisher that does not work with libraries, the library's only option is to buy that book, put it on an eReader, and loan the reader to the patron. The legality of loaning eReaders is still unclear, and the access to enhanced content becomes more and more difficult. If the library has only a few eReaders and they're loaded with enhanced eBooks, the ability to keep a small library on one device becomes a liability. These are just hypothetical situations, of course, and they don't even address the logistics of eReader-loaning programs or the difficulties of community ownership of personal devices. However, Becker is right that libraries view the digital divide as a major part of their mission and will continue to find and invent ways to bring eBooks to their patrons.

ACCESSIBILITY

Accessibility is an area of particular concern to librarians. Libraries typically offer tools and assistance to ensure accessibility of information to all their patrons. One of the frequently touted benefits of eReaders is the ability to increase the text size, a feature popular with baby boomers and older adults who have either relied on or been reluctant to transition to large-print books. However, eReaders are not as accessible as they might appear at first blush.

When the Kindle 2 debuted in 2009, it offered a text-to-speech option that read books in a computerized voice. The Authors Guild claimed that the feature violated copyright. Audiobooks are a lucrative business, and audio rights are considered separate from the copyright on the text. Writing in the *New York Times*, then-president of the Authors Guild Roy Blount Jr. said, "True, you can already get software that will read aloud whatever is on your computer. But Kindle 2 is being sold specifically as a new, improved, multimedia version of books—every title is an e-book and an audio book rolled into one. And whereas e-books have yet to win mainstream enthusiasm, audio books are a billion-dollar market, and growing. Audio rights are not generally packaged with e-book rights. They are more valuable than e-book rights. Income from audio books helps not inconsiderably to keep authors, and publishers, afloat" (Blount 2009). Amazon responded by allowing authors and publishers to opt into the text-to-speech on the Kindle. The NFB and the Reading Rights Coalition held a protest outside the offices of the Authors Guild.

Authors took issue with the Authors Guild, including Cory Doctorow, who said in a blog post, "This is nonsense, and I assume the AG knows it. First, because 'legally blind' is not the same as 'totally blind.' . . . Second, and most importantly: even if the Kindle had a big, Braille, 'I AM BLIND READ EVERYTHING ALOUD TO ME' button (thus rendering all its text accessible to even legally blind people), the Authors Guild's legal theories would *still* prohibit its production" (Doctorow 2009).

In a March 2009 letter to Simon & Schuster, the NFB and the International Dyslexia Association summed up the importance of accessible eBooks: "For a terribly long time those with print disabilities have been consigned to alternative formats with limited choices on expensive special purpose machines. Now that the opportunity for mainstream access to books on equal terms is possible, this community will not allow publishers and authors to deny them the right to read" (Engleman 2009). The groups also sent letters to the other Big Six publishers. They cited the multitude of state statutes that the Authors Guild was asking publishers and Amazon to potentially violate: "Should the publishing industry and Amazon accede to the Authors Guild's stance and deny persons with disabilities the service of mobile access to e-books it offers to the public, they will be at risk of violating state civil rights laws that guarantee equal access to persons with disabilities, including the Massachusetts Equal Rights Act, California's Unruh Act, the New Jersey Law Against Discrimination, and the Kentucky Civil Rights Act" (Engleman 2009).

In June of 2009, the NFB and the American Council of the Blind filed a suit against Arizona State University to stop the school from using Kindle DX to distribute eBooks. The two organizations also filed complaints with the Office for Civil Rights of the Department of Education and the Civil Rights Division of the Department of Justice against five other colleges and universities with Kindle DX pilot programs (Petri 2012, 55) created in conjunction with Amazon ("Justice Department Reaches Three Settlements"). By January of 2010, three of the schools had agreed not to purchase eReaders unless the devices were accessible. The Department of Justice, NFB, American Council of the Blind, and Arizona State University also reached a similar agreement ("Settlement Agreement").

In 2012, four blind patrons with the backing of the National Federation of the Blind sued the Free Library of Philadelphia because of a Nook-lending program for patrons over 50 (Schwartz 2012). According to a press release from the NFB, "the Free Library of Philadelphia is aware that the NOOK devices are inaccessible, and library personnel have openly discouraged two of the blind plaintiffs from even attempting to check out one of the devices. The library is also aware that it is violating federal laws, having been so advised by the United States Department of Education" ("National Federation of the Blind Assists" 2012). As of this writing, the litigation is still pending.

Currently, the eBook and eReader market has not provided the utopia of accessibility that seemed possible when eBooks first hit the mainstream. A January 2012 article in *The Braille Monitor* proves enlightening, if depressing. Surprisingly, the article rates Blio badly. Despite its origins with the NFB, Amy Mason finds that "while well intentioned and technologically impressive, Blio seems to have gotten so wrapped up in the final product and its visual presentation that many accessibility details have been overlooked or poorly implemented" (Mason 2012). She also discusses serious flaws in OverDrive and Adobe Digital Editions that make library eBooks extremely difficult to use. Google Books lands somewhere in the middle: "The Google Books reading experience is certainly better than a number of other options on this list, but a user has to play by Google's rules to get the system to work, and some accessibility barriers to purchasing books from the website still exist" (Mason 2012). The Nook is entirely inaccessible, highlighting the gulf between file format and end user. "Unprotected EPUB files are accessible primarily because they are built to be navigated very much like HTML documents. They contain similar structural elements, and, if the reader being used is accessible, the book is likely to be accessible as well unless it contains inaccessible charts, mathematical formulas, or illustrations," and the coming ePub3 format contains provisions to enhance accessibility (Mason 2012). The Kindle has not improved much for print-disabled people since 2009. "The Kindle 3 hardware reader and Kindle for PC with accessibility plugin (another specialized download) are the only confirmed options for reading Kindle materials with text-to-speech. Kindle on iOS and Mac are inaccessible to VoiceOver. Older Kindle hardware readers do not allow for text-to-speech control of the menus, and in the case of the least expensive Kindle ($79) or the recently released Kindle Fire, there are no accessibility features whatsoever. Text-to-speech can be turned off by the publisher on the Kindle 3, so not even all content can be accessed" (Mason 2012). Kindle for PC is "a slightly better experience" but still not for "anything but the most casual reading." Apple fares the best in Mason's assessment. Once a user owns an iOS device, "iBooks is one of the most accessible options available for reading commercial e-books today" (Mason 2012).

The state of affairs for mainstream eBook accessibility is disappointing. There are national and international efforts to improve accessibility, but they may have little impact on the American eBook market. The Association of American Publishers endorsed a United Nations (UN) project that "will explore the viability of a license-based worldwide exchange of copyrighted books in formats accessible for people who are blind, visually-impaired or have other print disabilities" (Sporkin 2011). The Trusted Intermediary Global Accessible Resources (TIGAR) pilot project is coordinated by the

> Currently, efforts from organizations like the NFB, the Reading Rights Coali-
> tion, and the International Dyslexia Association are providing the loudest
> voice for accessible eBooks. Library organizations have taken up the cause;
> ALA past-president Roberta Stevens appointed a task force, Equitable
> Access to Electronic Content (EQUACC), which made its final recommen-
> dations at the 2011 ALA Annual Conference. EQUACC notes on its website
> that both the Chief Officers of State Library Agencies (COSLA) and the
> Urban Libraries Council are working on accessibility issues and cites col-
> laboration with other ALA committees and task forces. Additionally, individ-
> ual champions of accessibility provide resources. After contributing a
> chapter to Sue Polanka's *No Shelf Required 2*, Ken Petri developed a
> website with resources on accessibility criteria and the accessibility features
> of various eReaders and eBook formats (http://wac.osu.edu/ebook-access-
> overview/). For librarians looking for real-world accessibility information,
> user reviews abound online. From articles like Amy Mason's to blog posts
> about eReader test drives, there is plenty of practical usability advice from
> those who need accessibility features. Colorado State University Libraries
> also produced a report on the accessibility of various eReaders: http://lib
> .colostate.edu/publicwiki/images/4/42/2011-02-07_FINAL_Report_—
> _Accessiblity_of_eBook_Readers.pdf. While we may not be able to offer
> completely accessible eBooks to our patrons yet, we can offer ideas and
> resources to make electronic content as accessible as possible.

UN's World Intellectual Property Organization (WIPO) and "is the result of
close collaboration between the World Intellectual Property Organization
(WIPO) and organizations representing VIPs, authors and publishers, namely
the World Blind Union (WBU), the International Federation of Library Asso-
ciations and Institutions (IFLA), the Digital Accessible Information System
(DAISY) Consortium, the International Publishers Association (IPA) and the
International Federation of Reproduction Rights Organisations (IFRRO)"
("Background"). The three-year project is working with publishers, advocacy
groups, and libraries to share accessible content, though the implementation
strategy for the project says that "in due course" end users will be able to
"search for and access adapted content" from commercial providers
("TIGAR Objectives and Implementation Strategy").

PRIVACY

Patron privacy is close to the heart of librarians, who often value it more
than the patrons do themselves. Librarians have struggled to find the line
between adhering to a core principle of our profession and paternalism.
Anyone who has worked in a library has doubtless come up against an
aggravated patron who wants to know the title of the book his or her spouse
has on hold or what his or her teenager has checked out at the moment.

The library community (and I'm including vendors here as well) has worked hard to offer features patrons want without compromising privacy. Our OPACs might have "if you liked x, you'll also enjoy y" features, but those data are compiled only after stripping patron information out. Patrons often assume that the library has a record of everything they've read and are surprised to find that the library doesn't want to hang on to that information. Many of our OPACs, however, feature an opt-in reading history that can be accessed only by patrons. We have sought to preserve privacy as we enhance our services, and when it comes to physical materials circulating via an integrated library system, we have been able to make decisions that achieve something of a balance.

eBooks are currently distributed primarily through third-party vendors. For a public library patron borrowing an eBook from OverDrive, there are two vendors involved: OverDrive and Adobe. Both have stated that they do not retain patrons' names (Kelley 2011g). Adobe tracks only the number of devices associated with a particular Adobe ID, not the content transferred to those devices. OverDrive does not retain any personal information, other than an eMail used to notify patrons of holds, and library card numbers (Kelley 2011g).

Once OverDrive added Kindle compatibility, the privacy picture changed. Patrons are directed to Amazon's site and required to log in to their Amazon accounts. While patrons with Kindles are already sharing their book-buying habits with Amazon, this requires them to share their book-borrowing habits as well. It also means that the library is providing a fundamental service—loaning books—without the standard library ethics and guidelines. Librarians are in the strange position of promoting a service to patrons and then warning of the privacy implications of that service. Nevertheless, although libraries can't attest to Amazon's privacy practices, they should at least be clear to their patrons that eBook loaning is not always managed entirely by the library. Gary Price, writing about the questions raised by OverDrive's partnership with Amazon, summed the issue up well, saying that

> We need to be providing clear and accessible disclosure and transparency with users for the service (and all other services) where an individual's data leaves the library's control ... We share books, serials, audio, video, and other information. And we *must* be sharing as clearly as possible what happens to a user's data—and let our users know when any service may compromise the level of privacy they've come to expect and appreciate from their library.
>
> *Finally, while I'm writing about Amazon.com today, issues with any third parties having access to library user data need to be discussed not only in the library community but also directly with users.* (emphasis his; Price 2011)

The law has historically been on the side of libraries and patron privacy. In an article in the *Huffington Post*, bookstore owner William Petrocelli cites two prominent cases where bookstores were able to keep buying records private. The first was Kenneth Starr's subpoena to a Washington, DC, bookstore for Monica Lewinsky's book purchases. The second was in Colorado, where The Tattered Cover bookstore received a warrant for the purchasing records of a suspect in a drug case (Petrocelli 2012). These cases involved brick-and-mortar bookstores and print books. However, the information available with digital book buying is greater than which titles are purchased. Sellers can see which books were browsed, looked at, purchased, or read, which pages were read more often, marginalia, and so on. In response to this technological change, California recently passed the California Reader Privacy Act, which went into effect on January 1, 2012. Petrocelli highlights the act's requirement that a bookseller "shall not knowingly disclose to any government entity, or be compelled to disclose to any person, private entity, or government entity, any personal information of a user" (California Senate Bill No. 602) without notice and a court order. Petrocelli adds that "it applies mainly to criminal cases, but it also applies in civil matters in which an enterprising attorney might issue a subpoena for evidence in, say, a tax case or a divorce case. The Act is an important first step, but it still leaves some pretty big holes in reader privacy" (Petrocelli 2012). Libraries can and should work with vendors to ensure patron privacy, but as the boundaries between the consumer eBook market and the library eBook market blur, our best bet for ensuring patron privacy may be to lobby our representatives to protect readers, regardless of where their book came from.

CHAPTER 8

Problem Solvers

At ALA Annual in 2009, I was asked what the future of libraries is. As a general rule, I avoid prognostication. It's too easy to be hung up on a current problem or potential solution and to be blindsided by a black-swan cultural shift or event. The most I felt comfortable saying was that I think libraries will find increasingly local solutions to universal problems. I still think that's likely to be true. When it comes to eBooks, most libraries are working with cookie-cutter products, though the local attitudes toward eBooks plays a big role. Among the libraries I work with, libraries in wealthier communities tend to participate in our consortial OverDrive collection and buy titles of their own through OverDrive's Advantage program, which lets consortium participants buy their own collection on top of the shared titles. Their patrons are demanding eBooks, and they're responding in the most cost-effective way they have. I also work with smaller libraries in less-well-off towns where the library is the place where people will likely first encounter an eBook. Patrons come in asking "What's all the fuss about?," and the library is there with refurbished eReaders and tablets for them to play with.

The libraries and librarians that get the most attention, though, are those that truly break out of the mold. There are several notable organizations that are making headlines in libraryland for their innovative solutions.

DOUGLAS COUNTY'S PARTNERSHIP WITH INDIE PUBLISHERS

In March of 2011, two Colorado libraries announced a new partnership with the Colorado Independent Publishers Association (CIPA). Douglas

County Libraries and Red Rocks Community College agreed to loan all of CIPA's titles and offer a link so that library patrons can purchase the eBook or print versions of the books (Rosen 2011). The libraries intended to not only purchase the eBooks but also manage the one-at-a-time loan of the books as well as supply their own DRM (Goldberg 2011). In July 2011, CIPA announced that the first books were available for loan through the library (CIPA Bookshelf 2011).

Jamie LaRue, director of the Douglas County Libraries, reports that the CIPA eBooks are "circulating briskly" and that he hopes to attract more publishers to partnerships with libraries like this one. The CIPA partnership was intended as a pilot project to "help us grow the knowledge we need to manage e-content ourselves and help us understand the issues our publisher partners might have," according to LaRue. The CIPA titles taught the library how to "massage, catalog, and integrate the content into our Integrated Library System [ILS]" (LaRue 2011).

Douglas County Libraries have their own server to host the eBooks, and they manage the DRM with Adobe. The titles are directly downloadable through the library catalog, and the records include links to buy books at a local bookstore or Amazon. eBooks can be read in the browser or transferred to a device, which LaRue said is still "awkward, depending on the device. But it's still easier than OverDrive" (LaRue 2011).

The library also has eBooks from the public domain, which are kept on a separate server. The Adobe Content Management server charges 8¢ per circulation to the library, so LaRue keeps anything that is freely available on a different machine.

LaRue suggested that for this model to succeed on a larger scale, libraries would have to form new consortia (LaRue 2011). This pilot project involves one library working with a publishing association to offer eBooks to library users. Publishers and libraries don't have the staff or resources to hammer out contracts on a one-to-one basis. Although this pilot project has been successful, it can't scale without purchasing consortia.

This project garnered attention as the first library-run eBook program. At the *Library Journal* Ebook Summit, "Ebooks: The New Normal," Monique Sendze, associate director of information technology at Douglas County Libraries, showed the library's "Powerwall," a display of new and popular titles in each library. She said the Powerwalls account for 60 percent of the circulation at their libraries. Douglas County is creating a digital Powerwall for their eBooks. The library uses VuFind, an open-source discovery layer, for their OPAC and has been able to extend that to showcase their eBooks. The digital Powerwalls allow patrons to browse the library's eBook collection, including those from OverDrive and 3M, place holds, check out eBooks to their accounts, as well as access their library accounts (Sendze 2011).

Douglas County also has "Buy Now" links on the books in their catalog. Patrons can buy books from Amazon, Barnes & Noble, or the Tattered

Douglas County has a YouTube video describing their Digital Branch: http:// youtu.be/uCWqiqRTupQ.

Library director Jamie LaRue blogs about the library and eBooks and posts regular updates about their innovative projects: http://jaslarue .blogspot.com/.

Other libraries are adopting the Douglas County model, including California's largest library network, the Califa Group, as well as Colorado's Marmot Library Network, Anythink Libraries in Colorado, and Wake County Public Libraries in North Carolina (Enis 2012b).

Cover, a Colorado independent bookstore. At Digital Book World 2012, Sendze said that between January 1, 2012, and January 23, 2012, the Buy Now buttons had been clicked 10,000 times. She added that in 2011, Douglas County eBook circulation went up 150 percent and print circulation dropped for the first time in 20 years. She called for more models for eBooks in libraries, asking the audience to imagine what their eBook circulation would be if they had access to all publishers' content and suggesting that a pay-per-use model could benefit everyone.

While Douglas County's partnerships with small publishers may not be something larger publishers would agree to, their success with eBooks, with offering patrons a way to buy books, and with owning their own electronic content serves as an important data point for libraries. Publisher-librarian collaboration can benefit both parties without causing a loss of sales or a rash of piracy. Although adopting this model is time consuming for the library, it allows for ownership of digital materials and a library-managed interface for patrons. Even if Douglas County is the only library able to achieve this level of success with their model, it represents an important building block for libraries and robust digital collection.

ANN ARBOR'S DIY APPROACH

Eli Neiburger has famously said that libraries are screwed (Neiburger 2010). As eBook costs drop, ads become commonplace, and books become "book thingies" packaged with other goods, the library's role becomes unclear to its users (Neiburger 2011a). The library is (ostensibly) free, but so are apps, which don't show up on a town's or university's budget. As many public librarians know, casting the library as free can lead to some confusion when the library asks for funding, through either taxes or donations. As free and freemium (as in games that are free, but offer purchases within the confines of the app) become the standard for media purchases, the library's "free," with its accompanying tax or tuition bill, loses both clarity and appeal.

How does the library survive, then? It's worth noting that Neiburger works at a library well known for its successful innovations; and the idea that the associate director for IT and production of a busy, well-respected library keeps saying that libraries are screwed can be a bit disheartening, if not downright upsetting. But what Ann Arbor District Library (AADL) has done is to look for ways the library can create wonderful, valuable experiences for its community. The bulk of the library's eBook collection comes from a cooperative buying group, the Midwest Collaborative for Library Services, which uses OverDrive. The library's true innovation is not in how it buys eBooks, but in how it partners with the community to create its own content and local collections.

AADL's programs place heavy emphasis on creation. Sometime it's creation by an expert, as in the case of the puppet and green-screen movie maker who presented a program on how he makes his movies, complete with audience participation. In the case of the green-screen presentation, audience members were brought up to the front of the room to participate in the demonstration of green-screen technology. More often, the library's members are the creators, as in the annual LEGO-building contest sponsored by the library. The library also digitizes not only their own local history materials but also those of town residents, including an unusual tray with an image of Ann Arbor on it that was owned by a local resident (Neiburger 2011a). The library gives residents digital versions of their treasures, but is also able to expand their local history collection to include things previously seen only by their owners. Those newspapers, photos, and videos are accessible by the general public only through AADL, as are their podcasts and other more recent local creations (Neiburger 2011a).

Unique collections need not be only local materials. Neiburger suggests loaning out objects that hit a "sweet spot" of medium cost, short duration of use, and a low frequency of use (Neiburger 2011a). Many libraries already loan out items like tools, cake pans, musical instruments, and puppets, all of which meet his criteria. Engagement with library members is also key to Neiburger's vision. AADL gives out badges and points as part of its summer reading program, much like sites like GetGlue and apps like FourSquare, which reward users for "checking in" to locations activities, as well as consuming media like television shows and movies. The range of services and methods of connecting with their members, Neiburger argues, will help the library retain value for taxpayers regardless of the eBook future (Neiburger 2011a).

What Neiburger has advocated for repeatedly is for libraries to make themselves valuable to their communities in ways that are not book related. The eBook future is unclear to everyone, and it's being driven by market forces that don't take libraries into account or are actively hostile to library interests. The way to stay relevant is not shout to be heard over Amazon, but to deepen the library's ties to its community by engaging with the people the library serves.

This approach is nearly poetic in its love of library and community, but Ann Arbor is well positioned to pursue this ideal. The city is home to five colleges and universities and boasts a well-educated population. The library has been crafting innovative and engaging programs for years—this is not so much their response to eBooks, but their vision for what the twenty-first-century library should look like. The library's emphasis in programs and digital media is on local talent (Morgan 2011), which is abundant in Ann Arbor. For libraries in communities dissimilar to Ann Arbor, these projects can seem impossible. The principle is what's important—a variety of connections to the community serve as a way of rising above the tumultuous world of rapidly changing technology. That's not to say that technology isn't important, but what Neiburger does at Ann Arbor is to incorporate emerging technology that the Ann Arbor community is using into local, community-centered library programs and services.

A local approach resonates with both library users and potential funding sources. As Jessamyn West has said when talking about the digital divide, "Local is often fundable" (West 2011b). Libraries that pursue grants for local history projects or seek funding to address a specific community concern are often successful. Projects that create partnerships with other organizations build library visibility and community stature. In a talk entitled "What If the Future . . . (Is Like the Past)?," Peter Brantley of the Internet Archive also touched on this idea, saying that it is "not mad for libraries to 'write off' ebooks and focus on services that will be attractive in the future" (Brantley 2011). He cites library projects like Chicago's YouMedia, a "teen learning space" that's a part of Chicago Public Library, and suggests partnerships with community projects like Berkeley's hyperlocal news outlet Berkeleyside (Brantley 2011).

Libraries are still identified very strongly with books. Books have been our brand since they become the dominant information technology (and it was scrolls and lengths of parchment before that). Librarians, especially when seeking funding, argue that the library is really about access to information. What AADL and others who share their philosophy are creating is a library that emphasizes creation. Community members might head into the library to pick up a novel to read and while they're there discover that the library offers ways for them to tell their own stories, create their own content.

This philosophy requires a change how libraries benchmark. Circulation statistics have long been the standard by which libraries gauge success. Programming brought people into the library so they would then check out materials. As libraries have expanded beyond book-related programming, the "get them in the door to get them to check things out" strategy has become less tenable. "Creation" is becoming an important watchword for libraries. Libraries are offering self-publishing services, 3-D printers, and other tools for creation. Writing about the "Made in a Library" symposium, Matt Enis observed that "libraries could serve as a point of collaboration for creativity within a community, and could help spark it by purchasing equipment like 3D printers, which, starting at about $1800, are out of reach for all but the most dedicated hobbyists, but are much less expensive for a library to provide" (Enis 2012c). At libraries like Ann Arbor, librarians are getting patrons in the door and engaged with the library; picking up that novel is secondary to giving the community a voice.

LIBRARY RENEWAL

Library Renewal is the brainchild of librarian Michael Porter, who began work on the organization in 2008. Porter "didn't see anyone creating anything that would work for rights holders, readers, and libraries"(Porter 2011) when it came to digital objects. He realized that the problem was not a technical one, but one of infrastructure. Legal issues, control of pricing, and relationships between libraries and other stakeholders all have an impact on the infrastructure Library Renewal hopes to help create. To that end, Library Renewal is a nonprofit dedicated to improving both access to electronic content for library patrons, and the economics of eBooks for libraries (Porter 2012).

Library Renewal's work has four components: research, developing relationships, creating partnerships, and finding solutions. Their goal is to create a platform for electronic content access that's by libraries, for libraries, and with libraries. Porter says their process will be transparent, and Library Renewal expects to be able to pay rights holders more, while costing libraries less, as there will not be any markup on their electronic content. This, says Porter, will be an entirely new system, one that does not imitate the print model (Porter 2012).

The nonprofit works with a group of partner libraries that act as an advisory board, providing the staff and board of Library Renewal with feedback as well as holding the organization true to its mission of "by libraries, for libraries, with libraries." Partner libraries generally don't contribute funding, but do volunteer five hours of staff time a month to planning meetings and projects. Library Renewal also works with both partner and nonpartner libraries on related projects, like securing grants and working on strategic planning for eContent and digital strategies. Library Renewal hopes to offer a home for the work being done by librarians preparing for a digital future, in part by providing services that eliminate the need to start from scratch when planning at the local level. For example, libraries that may be interested in emulating Douglas County's approach to eBooks could work with Library Renewal to plan, fund, and build their own eBook-lending platform. While that wouldn't be a national solution, Library Renewal could act as a coordinating body between libraries pursuing local solutions. Eventually, that could build to the organization's grand vision (Porter 2012).

Library Renewal's board members are an impressive group, and their shared blog offers interesting insights into and ideas about eBooks and eBook news. This model is, arguably, the ideal for libraries, with more in common with our print book purchasing and less with electronic journal subscriptions. Library-driven solutions are few and far between, while eBook vendors are cropping up regularly. While a competitive marketplace will benefit libraries, a platform run by a library co-op could very well be the healthiest eBook solution for libraries. As always, the key is content and compatibility. Without popular content and eReader compatibility, public libraries will be closed out of the eBook ecosystem.

The vision of Library Renewal is admirable, and the organization is worthy of library support. However, without funding, it will remain only a vision. I asked Michael Porter if he had considered pursuing venture capital funding, though that would likely require the nonprofit to restructure as a for-profit undertaking. He said that while the funding offered by venture capitalists was tempting, both potential funders and the board had found that the only way the organization would work was as a nonprofit that would keep costs as low as possible while reinvesting in access to eBooks rather than repaying venture funders (Porter 2012). This isn't surprising given the library-driven mission of the organization and the tendency among librarians to value and trust nonprofits more than for-profit companies.

In addition to their blog, Library Renewal plans to expand their education and outreach initiatives. Porter notes that the blog includes weekly eContent news summaries and that the board and other volunteers will be offering regular webinars on eBook issues. Although every librarian is aware of eBooks, Porter says that it's important for librarians to understand the magnitude of their impact, saying "We believe that libraries equal content plus community. If we can't offer the econtent people want and need, our value, significance and support will dwindle drastically. That can't be allowed to happen" (Porter 2012).

GLUEJAR

Another recent entrant into the eBook world is Eric Hellman's brainchild, unglue.it. Like Library Renewal, the goal is to fairly compensate authors and publishers while freeing eBooks for the public to use. However, Gluejar is not strictly a library platform. The model for the company is deceptively simple: the rights holder works with Gluejar to set a fair price for "ungluing" a book, that is, making the eBook freely available to readers online. Readers contribute to the books that they want to generate a lump-sum payment to the rights holder. When a book has been unglued, it will be offered through the site with a Creative Commons license ("Vision"). The site launched on May 17, 2012. When it was in preview, users could create wish lists of books that they want to unglue, but couldn't pledge money yet. When it launched, it featured a handful of campaigns for books with funding thresholds between $5,000 and $25,000 (Enis 2012a). The site's launch was noted by Cory Doctorow on Boing Boing, specifically drawing attention to the campaign to unglue *Oral Literature in Africa*, which Doctorow said was sought after by African libraries (Doctorow 2012b). Oral Literature in Africa was unglued and made available for download in September 2012.

Ideally, says Gluejar's librarian Andromeda Yelton, Gluejar will save libraries time and money by making content more freely available without gatekeepers (Yelton 2011). It seems likely that Gluejar will have success at first with less-well-known authors and titles, and then with niche audiences. In *The No Shelf Required Guide to E-book Purchasing*, Hellman offers the example of a romance series author. The rights to the earlier books in the series have reverted to the author, but she doesn't have the money or mechanism to convert them to eBook format. Using a site like Gluejar, she can release the first book under a Creative Commons license for a payment she considers to be fair. Alternatively, a reader can suggest a title and fans can pledge support until the lump sum is large enough for the rights holder to take notice (Hellman 2011b, 24). Yelton is working on a toolkit for publishers to reach out to the community around a book, to help unlock the passion surrounding a title to be unglued (Yelton 2011). The success of sites like Kickstarter have shown that crowdfunding can work well. However, in the case of Kickstarter and other similar sites, the people asking for funding are the creators themselves. In this case, Gluejar has the difficult task of negotiating payment with authors and publishers. This task was made more difficult by Amazon Payments suspended work with crowdsourcing organizations like Gluejar, a road bump detailed without rancor by Gluejar founder Eric Hellman on his blog (Hellman 2012). Like Library Renewal, the team at the company is impressive (and they also have excellent blogs), but they, too, have a gargantuan task ahead of them.

Both Gluejar and Library Renewal could greatly benefit libraries, but their long-term impact remains to be seen. As with Douglas County, even if only smaller publishers and less-popular works are offered to libraries or unglued for all readers, the advocacy for alternative models that Library Renewal and Gluejar have spearheaded is important. As publishers and librarians move forward with eBook-lending systems, the more possibilities for libraries and library advocates to offer a variety of eBook buying and borrowing models, the greater the likelihood that libraries will end up with a sustainable eBook ecosystem.

OPEN LIBRARY

The Internet Archive, home of librarian favorite The Wayback Machine, was founded in 1996 to build an Internet library. Wary of losing websites and other digital content as the Internet grew, the Internet Archive saves the content of the Internet because "without cultural artifacts, civilization has no memory and no mechanism to learn from its successes and failures. And paradoxically, with the explosion of the Internet, we live in what Danny Hillis has referred to as our 'digital dark age'" ("About the Internet Archive").

Open Library is an initiative of the Internet Archive, with a stated goal of creating one web page for every book. As of this writing, they have 20 million records. The project is open, meaning the software used to create it is open source, and the records are open to anyone who wants to contribute. As on Project Gutenberg, books that are out of copyright are also available to read, but the Open Library's goal is simply to have a page for every book. In March 2011, Open Library began a lending program for libraries. Libraries send copies of books to the Internet Archive, which then digitizes them and makes them available to patrons of participating libraries (Kelley 2011a). Copyrighted books are available only to people in the library that owns the book. Open Library uses IP authentication to ensure that those downloading the eBook are doing so over the library's network. Once the book is digitized, the Internet Archive will either store it or return it to the library, though they recommend that the library keep the paper book from being lent, in order to bolster a fair use argument for this eBook approach (Kelley 2011a).

In October 2011, COSLA voted unanimously to "enter into a memorandum of understanding with the Internet Archive...that will essentially make the state librarian in each state a point person for the Open Library's lending program" (Kelley 2011a). COSLA members expressed concern about a study COSLA conducted showing that 40 percent of public libraries are not offering eBooks (Kelley 2011a).

The Open Library plan could open eBooks up to a larger number of public libraries, and prominent librarians have happily endorsed it. The Librarian in Black, Sarah Houghton, calls it "freaking awesome" (Houghton 2011b); and Jessamyn West says it is "an example of both a project that is nice and library like while also being attractive and usable and, at the same time, pushing the envelope of 'how to be a library' in ways that are dignifying to both patrons and librarians alike" (West 2011c). Open Library maintains a stats page showing the growing popularity of their content, which libraries have the most loans, the average time a book is checked out for (1 day is the most popular right now, followed by 15 days), and popular titles, among other things. There are over a million free eBooks in the Open Library, an additional 100,000 available to people borrowing from within one of the 1,000 participating libraries. The list of eBooks available to people in participating libraries does include newer titles, though many of them are protected DAISY files that cannot be accessed without a key issued by the Library of Congress. DAISY stands for *Digital Accessible Information SYstem* and is a set of standards for making text accessible to those who can't read print ("DAISY Demystified").

This project may, as Houghton suggests, be the future of libraries. So far, Open Library's interpretation of fair use has gone unchallenged. As COSLA members begin sending materials and more libraries begin marketing the service to their patrons, lawsuits seem inevitable. At ALA Midwinter 2012, a panel of legal experts "urged librarians to go forth and digitize, that they already have the sturdy legal cover they need to proceed: *fair use*" (Albanese 2012a). The Internet Archive's global director of books said that the organization has not been sued yet for the Open Library initiative because " 'libraries have been handling in-copyright material for years. . . . [borrowers] authenticate as patron, the patron takes the book off the shelf, the patron brings it back.' The key for transferring this to the digital realm, Miller explained, was to ensure no more than one copy circulates at a time, a mission they take so seriously that the physical books from which the scans are created are sealed in shipping containers and stored in a warehouse" (Albanese 2012a). At first blush, Open Library seems a little crazy, like begging for litigation, but as libraries continue to partner with Internet Archive, it could just look like eBook salvation.

DPLA AND HATHITRUST

Digital Public Library of America

The Digital Public Library of America (DPLA) is a project based at Harvard University's Berkman Center for Internet & Society. The project is backed by the Alfred P. Sloan Foundation and is currently working toward an April 2013 launch date. The development team released its first build, which they called "highly tentative" (Weinberger 2012) on February 1, 2012. The planners hold regular open meetings to discuss the project and often stream the meetings online for those who can't make the trip to the meeting location. The project has not been without controversy. During one of the early plenary meetings, a Twitter wag joked that the only word in Digital Public Library of America that hadn't been debated was "of." The DPLA "About" page states "Although many different opinions exist as to the characteristics of the ultimate deliverable, the DPLA, all agree that our goal is to create a resource that goes well beyond providing simple access to digitized or born digital content" ("Elements of the DPLA").

The project has an active (if occasionally overwhelming) main list serv that is open for anyone to join, and workstream list servs for each of the defined areas of interest. In 2011, DPLA put out a call for "Beta Sprint" participants to submit "ideas, models, prototypes, technical tools, user interfaces, etc.—put forth as a written statement, a visual display, code, or a combination of forms—that demonstrate how the DPLA might index and provide access to a wide range of broadly distributed content. The Beta Sprint also encourages development of submissions that suggest alternative designs or that focus on particular parts of the system, rather than on the DPLA as a whole" ("Digital Public Library of America Steering Committee Announces" 2011). Selected Beta Sprint participants were asked to present their ideas at a public plenary meeting, and their presentations were posted on the DPLA website.

The content of the DPLA is starting with public-domain works, but will expand to orphan works and those that are in copyright but out of print. The project will "explore models for digital lending of in-copyright materials" ("Elements of the DPLA"), but since the DPLA is in its infancy, it is impossible to say what those models might look like. For some, projects like DPLA offer a tremendous possibility. At a forum held in October 2011 to discuss the pros and cons of DPLA, Harvard University library director Robert Darnton held out hope that "where Google failed, the DPLA can succeed . . . It can draw on a huge database of already digitized material from HathiTrust, the Internet Archive, the Library of Congress, research libraries (Harvard has digitized and made available 2.3 million titles), and state libraries. Darnton suggested starting with these special collections and titles in the public domain, leaving out current materials and orphan works (in-copyright titles[,] titles for whom copyright holders cannot be found)" ("Digital Public Library of America: Pro and Con" 2011). However, the emphasis on public domain works and special collections "seems to belie his statement that DPLA 'will serve all spectrums of society . . . from pre-K on up.' In fact, one criticism of the DPLA is that because it will not include current popular books, it cannot serve public library users" ("Digital Public Library of America: Pro and Con" 2011).

HathiTrust

A reticence to include current popular books is somewhat understandable given the experience of the HathiTrust. HathiTrust is a digital library created by a partnership of "major research institutions and libraries working to ensure that the cultural record is preserved and accessible long into the future" ("Welcome to the Shared Digital Future"). The organization digitizes works that are under copyright, but provides access only "to those publications where permitted by law or by the rights holder" ("Copyright"). The collection passed 10 million volumes on January 5, 2012, with more than 2.7 million of those items in the public domain (Kelley 2012c). Preservation is a key component of the HathiTrust project. In an interview in *Library Journal*, Heather Christenson, the mass digitization project manager and HathiTrust project manager at the California Digital Library, said, "One of the most important distinctions is that HathiTrust has a *stated intention* to preserve digital volumes over the long term. Our goal is for the researcher to be able to use these items in 20 years, 50 years, and onward" (Booth 2011).

However, in September of 2011 the Authors Guild, the Australian Society of Authors, a Canadian writer's union, and eight authors sued HathiTrust, the University of Michigan (where the HathiTrust infrastructure is hosted), the University of California, Cornell University, Indiana University, and the University of Wisconsin ("Authors Guild Sues HathiTrust and 5 Other Universities Over Digitized Books"). At the heart of the suit is HathiTrust's collaboration with Google, alleging that "HathiTrust is built with millions of 'unauthorized' scans created by Google. The suit seeks an injunction barring the libraries from future digitization of copyrighted works; from providing works to Google for its scanning project; and from proceeding with its plan to allow access to 'orphan works.' It also asks the court to 'impound' all unauthorized scans and to hold them in escrow 'pending an appropriate act of Congress' " (Albanese 2011). HathiTrust, for its part has stated that "we do not plan to change our access and preservation procedures in light of the lawsuit. We have a defined policy and process by which parties may contend the use of certain works, which will remain in play" ("Information about the Authors Guild Lawsuit"). Librarians have, of course, condemned the Authors Guild for the suit. Speaking to LJ, an intellectual property attorney, Jonathan Band disparaged the suit and questioned the Authors Guild's thinking "that Section 108 [of the Copyright Act] limits fair use" (Rapp 2011a). The trial is slated to start in November 2012 ("HathiTrust Answers Authors Guild Lawsuit").

The seemingly endless litigation associated with digitizing materials tends to give libraries, especially those without deep pockets, pause. Groups like DPLA and HathiTrust are determined to continue in their work, which, even if it doesn't provide current copyrighted material to public libraries, will benefit us all. Large-scale digitization of public-domain materials may not be as exciting as hot new bestsellers, but even popular reading libraries will find the historical materials available on HathiTrust's site useful and interesting. Commenting on the national-level efforts to digitize materials, Dan Fogel, technical lead for mass digitization and cotechnical lead for the HathiTrust at the University of California's California Digital Library, told Char Booth, "Ultimately it means that more users [sic] needs are served. Also, digital preservation—of the cultural record, of digitally born data—is a big deal. Libraries have long focused on preserving print collections and it only follows that they should also preserve digital materials. But preservation should be in the service of access and use. It is early days for the digital library, but it just isn't efficient that every library—school libraries, public libraries, academic libraries—has to build their own services" (Booth 2011).

These problem solvers all share a desire to find solutions that work for readers, authors, publishers, and libraries. None of them promote their project as the only way to offer eBooks, but rather as one of many paths forward. All of them can flourish simultaneously, which would be a fantastic situation for libraries. When you're considering eBook strategies for your library, you may find that none of these ideas are possible for you to emulate, but perhaps you could draw inspiration from Ann Arbor's dedication to local talent or approach a larger group of libraries in your area about working on a Douglas County-style eBook platform. Even adding links to HathiTrust, Open Library, or Gluejar to your website might generate conversation with your patrons and stakeholders. It may feel nearly impossible to strategize more than five minutes ahead when it comes to eBooks, but checking in with libraries and organizations that have forged their own paths might make the future seem a little brighter for the rest of us.

CHAPTER 9

Scenarios for the Future

WHAT DOES THE FUTURE HOLD?

Anyone who works with books knows that eBooks and publishing are changing rapidly, and at any moment, a new announcement from Amazon or game-changing gadget from Apple could alter the trajectory we're on. It would be foolish of me to offer any bold predictions of the future. I am happy to speculate, though, and share some of the scenarios that could play out.

THE FRAGMENTED MARKETPLACE

The fragmented marketplace is, to a greater or lesser extent, where we stand now. eReader and tablet owners exist in their own walled gardens. There are some small bridges—Apple's iOS and Android OS both allow for Nook and Kindle apps, though they lack many of the features of the actual devices. Although I am drawn to analogies of the early days of Mac/PC where moving between operating systems was next to impossible, it may be that these differences become more entrenched, not less. Apple's new iBooks for textbooks and Author software require schools to commit to Apple's platform. Writing about the lovely design of the textbook services, GigaOm's Matthew Ingram said, "As usual, all this great design requires a major trade-off: namely, that schools and publishers agree to be locked inside Apple's walled-garden ecosystem. That might be fine for music and movies and games like *Angry Birds*, but is that really appropriate for educational material?" (Ingram 2012).

The ePub standard is the saving grace, although Amazon doesn't use it and Apple might be moving away from it. Libraries can offer ePubs, and they'll work on a variety of readers. When OverDrive first announced their Kindle compatibility, the first question on many librarians' minds was "Will I have to buy another format?" Fortunately, the answer was no, but that answer could change in the future. We're beginning to see fragmentation not just in who will sell to libraries, but in how they price their eBooks. Random House will sell unfettered eBooks to libraries at a much higher cost, but other publishers won't sell to libraries at all. The price increases from Random House and now Hachette serve only to muddy the waters as libraries try to prove their value in the eBook (and book) market. The higher prices change libraries' demand and our patrons' supply. Random House has asked for data from libraries so they may assess the impact loans have on sales, but as Peter Brantley notes in Publishers Weekly, that data will not help Random House price their books. "First, variability in efficient market pricing for books is pronounced, dependent on title, genre, and audience profiles, making generalizations difficult. Additionally, market pricing is characterized by temporal fluctuation; most books are more valuable shortly after release . . . Finally, when auctions are initiated with an artificial pricing floor, poorer bidders—unable to accept sub-floor pricing—cannot influence the outcome. If a book auction starts at $85 and I can only pay $35, those who can afford $125 will propel pricing to a level beyond what the overall market would have otherwise determined" (Brantley 2012).

Publishers have struggled with eBook pricing, and not just to libraries. Prior to the move to the agency model, Amazon was pricing all their eBooks at $9.99, but publishers fought that price (even though wholesale pricing was more profitable for publishers) as it undermined pricing on print books (Gilmor 2011). That move, however, led to publishers and Apple being investigated for antitrust violations by the European Union, the DOJ, and the attorneys general of a number of states. "At issue is whether any antitrust violations occurred when Apple signed on several of the largest publishers to publish e-books through its iBookstore, which coincided with the launch of the iPad. Apple merely acts as an 'agent' for the publishers, selling e-books at whatever price the publisher sets. Apple then takes its customary 30 percent cut as it does with music, movies, and apps" (Foresman 2011).

eBook pricing for libraries is already all over the map, but it seems likely that it will get even more inconsistent, at least in the short run. Perhaps publishers that have previously not sold to libraries will start to, but only at elevated prices, or through a preferred platform. Penguin pulled their new titles from OverDrive because of issues with Amazon's presence in the library market (Hellman 2011a), but if 3M does not pursue Kindle compatibility, will Penguin titles be available there? Penguin's pilot project is with 3M, which could be related to their Kindleless status, or may be entirely unrelated. For consumers, Amazon's publishing program has meant that some eBooks are not going to be available through non-Amazon channels; in response to Amazon's publishing arm, Barnes & Noble has decided not to sell Amazon-published titles in their stores (Bosman 2012a). Amazon has deeper pockets, but Barnes & Noble has the floor space that publishers need. Indeed, lack of floor space may be a weakness for Amazon, one that physical retailers are starting to take advantage of; both Target and Wal-mart stopped selling Kindles in 2012 (Wohl 2012). Speaking to the *New York Times*, David Shaks, CEO of Penguin, said, " 'For all publishers, it's really important that brick-and-mortar retailers survive . . . Not only are they key to keeping our physical book business thriving, there is also the carry-on effect of the display of a book that contributes to selling e-books and audio books. The more visibility a book has, the more inclined a reader is to make a purchase' " (Bosman 2012b). This kind of retail fragmentation could continue, with Amazon specializing in its own content and Barnes & Noble serving more and more as a publishing showroom. For libraries, this could mean subscribing to multiple eBook vendors to access the widest variety of content or more windowing or other restrictions. For readers, the book marketplace is about to get a little bit stranger—Barnes & Noble employees may be getting a taste of the frustration librarians have felt in having to explain that certain publishers don't work with libraries.

THE MONOPOLY MARKETPLACE

Everyone's got an opinion about Amazon. They're the 800-pound gorilla of the eBook marketplace, and their influence is strong enough to make even the biggest publishers worry. The consumer allure is obvious: good prices on almost anything you might like to buy, delivered promptly. Personally, when I lived in an area full of local businesses and bookstores, where every bookseller and coffee shop offered used books for a few dollars each, I didn't shop from Amazon as frequently. A move to the suburbs where almost every store is a national chain and most shopping expeditions entail a trip to the mall (or the congested area around the mall) meant I was happy to pay for Prime membership and shop from Amazon regularly. Working on this book has made me less likely to buy from Amazon. Even though the nearest bookstore is a Barnes & Noble about 30 minutes away, not exactly a local business in any sense of the word, I've found myself disinclined to spend so much of my book-buying dollars at Amazon. It's not that I think the company is malicious, but like many in the book industry, I'm just nervous about their size and power.

Amazon is reportedly taking losses on both the Kindle (Poeter 2011) and, at least sometimes, Kindle books (Shatzkin 2011a). The sold-at-a-loss Kindles are the ad-supported versions, but the Kindle Fire is also being sold at a loss. *PC Magazine* cites research firm IHS's theory that "Amazon thinks the real money to be made via the Kindle Fire is through sales of all the other stuff the company sells that's completely unrelated to tablets or computing—everything from toilet paper to cribs to umbrellas. The Kindle Fire, the research firm theorized, is a portable, digital storefront for Amazon that steers users to pour more of their money into the company's multi-billion-dollar retail operation" (Poeter 2011). The latest generation of Kindles is also said to be generating very small or possibly no profits at all ("Amazon's New Kindle Will Have Thin Profit Margin"). This is more than simply selling the razors at a loss to get people locked in to the blades. DRM encourages platform loyalty in the eReader market, but only Amazon sells so much more than media.

Amazon also angered many consumers in December of 2011 with its Price Check promotion. The company offers an app for iPhones and Android phones that allows consumers to compare prices on an item in a brick-and-mortar retail store with Amazon's prices. For a brief window in December, Amazon was offering 5 percent discounts to consumers who used this app to make purchases from Amazon instead of physical stores. They were widely criticized; Gawker posted a story about it under the heading "Evil" and exhorted readers, "please don't do this cheap, sad thing" (Tate 2011). In exchange for the small discount, consumers were giving Amazon tremendous amounts of information about their shopping habits, something that Amazon specializes in—anyone who has received an eMail from Amazon after browsing for a potential purchase on the site knows how much Amazon knows about what we buy and what we think about buying.

Book enthusiasts point out that knowing what we buy doesn't mean that Amazon knows what we read or like, which is why Amazon's recommendations are decent enough, but not as good as a bookseller's or librarian's. However, Amazon is not in the discovery business, except insofar as it's in Amazon's best interests for customers to discover new things to buy. Amazon is interested in more than just publishing or tablets, and their direct contact with customers is one of their greatest strengths. In an open letter to the DOJ, Mike Shatzkin points out that Amazon's customer database goes far beyond book purchases and that imbalance means that "without uniform retail pricing, Amazon can effectively disintermediate the publishers, but the publishers can't effectively disintermediate Amazon" (Shatzkin 2012b). It's entirely possible to purchase all of your media, do all of your cultural consumption through Amazon, using Amazon-created devices. If you also use their cloud storage, that can include all of your cultural output. If you publish your work on Amazon, using either a self-publishing model or using Amazon as your publisher, you can make income off of that cultural output. Amazon has created an entire ecosystem that encompasses everything from books, music, and movies, to financial systems and cloud computing.

Publishers are wary of Amazon's might, and while the agency-pricing battle continues, publishers are also fighting Amazon on library lending. Amazon launched a lending library for Kindle owners with Amazon Prime memberships on November 3, 2011. Customers can borrow one book a month, with no due date. The collection of lendable titles started out with 5,000 items; but by the end of December 2011 it had reached 66,037 books, more than even active library eBook collections, as Michael Kelley writing on *Library Journal's Digital Shift* blog observed (Kelley 2011b). None of the Big Six publishers have chosen to have their books included in Amazon's lending, and the opposition to Amazon's library may have leaked over into opposition to lending eBooks through libraries. Kelley cites Penguin CEO John Makinson telling the Reuters Global Media Summit that "Amazon is embarking on new initiatives that could put file security at risk and that would be not good for anyone" (Kelley 2011b). Similarly, Penguin cited security concerns when it temporarily removed Kindle versions of Penguin books and stopped loaning new eBooks through OverDrive at the end of 2011.

Penguin's security concerns were never spelled out, but the decision to remove Kindle access to their books in OverDrive signaled that the concern was actually with Amazon, not with libraries. On his blog, *Go to Hellman*, Eric Hellman explained, "The Penguin move should be seen not as corporate verdict on libraries, but as a reaction to Amazon's entry into the library market. When Overdrive was distributing content to libraries on their own platform, the publishers were able to view Overdrive, and libraries in general, as a counterweight to Amazon. But the extension of Overdrive lending to the Kindle flipped libraries into the Amazon column. That's the best way to understand the Penguin decision, though you won't see them saying that" (Hellman 2011a). Amazon is already quite powerful and has the potential to become even more so.

Mike Shatzkin has theorized that the U.S. market for narrative text (books that are mostly text) will be 80 percent digital within the next two to five years (Shatzkin 2011e). He goes so far as to say that "when I say I think we'll hit it in two to five years, I'm being consciously restrained. To get there in two years would require that consumers switch from print to digital at about 60–70 percent of the speed they have for the last four years over the next two. Were it to take five years, it would mean the conversion rate would have slowed to a crawl compared to where it has been" (Shatzkin 2011c). The Kindle continues to dominate the eReader market, with consumers purchasing over 1 million Kindles a week during December 2011. Each recipient of a Kindle is, to a greater or lesser extent, locking themselves into Amazon's book ecosystem. So are Nook owners, but Nooks aren't as popular as Kindles, and Barnes & Noble isn't quite the cross-channel behemoth that Amazon is. How much of that 80 percent will be Amazon's share?

Harvard Business Review editor and blogger Sarah Green suggested in a December 27, 2011, post that Amazon should partner with independent bookstores. The picture she paints is charming for readers and a wonderful portrait of independent bookstores as a vital part of book culture. Discussing both displays and helpful booksellers, she says "that's why when I walk into a place like the Brookline Booksmith, City Lights, Politics and Prose, Powell's, or the Tattered Cover, I walk in wanting to buy nothing and soon want to buy ... everything" (Green 2011). She argues that Amazon needs physical bookstores, that "Amazon needs to accept that destroying the ecosystem of physical shops—both national chains and independent stores—destroys the ecosystem it needs to sustain itself in the long term" (Green 2011). She may be right when talking about print, but for a Kindle owner looking for a new book to download, purchases can't be shared between the physical bookstore and Amazon. Green also argues that Amazon's price check promotion proves that Amazon sees the value in physical shops to their bottom line, but it remains to be seen if that's something the company sees as having long-term value or if the price check promotion was simply a bid for consumer behavior data.

In many ways, the question is not "will Amazon have monopoly control over the book ecosystem?" but "to what extent will Amazon's monopoly dominate?" Will Amazon simply continue as the United States' largest bookseller and become one of many publishers or will Amazon dominate and recreate both publishing and bookselling?

LIBRARIES BECOME CANDLE MAKERS

At the 2010 *Library Journal/School Library Journal* Online Summit, "ebooks: Libraries at the Tipping Point," Eli Neiburger likened the future of books to candles. We still use candles, of course, but not as a primary light source. We're happy to pay far more for them than they cost (they're an extravagance, not a utility), and we like them to come in interesting shapes and smell nice and so on (Neiburger 2010). Already, publishers are wondering about things like illustrated books and art books and pop-up books and things that don't translate well to the screen just yet. Mike Shatzkin, writing about the future of illustrated books on small screens, observes, "As bookstore shelf space disappears, the urgency of solving this problem grows. The sales of illustrated books have reportedly been going up in the bookstores, which is good news for as long as it lasts. It makes complete sense that retailers would emphasize the things that seeing and touching make you more likely to buy. But I'd be concerned that even the sales of illustrated books will suffer as more and more of the straight text consumers find what they want without visiting a bookstore. And a closed bookstore doesn't sell any illustrated books at all" (Shatzkin 2011d).

Shatzkin is talking about bookstores, but of course, this applies to libraries as well. Books that don't work well on small screens (or any screens) are a growth market for anyone with shelf space. But for libraries, that kind of specialization might not sit well. We're about access to information, after all, not access to "stuff that doesn't look as pretty on a seven-inch screen." Libraries might also offer print on demand services, actually making the candles we loan out (or sell, as the case may be). That's less library-as-publisher and more library-as-printer, perhaps a less glamorous hat to wear. And, as Shatzkin points out, a shrinking niche market that people don't always know they're interested in isn't enough to keep the doors open. However, libraries do offer more than just books; as Tim Spalding (of LibraryThing) observes, libraries "do other solid, valuable things" (Spalding 2010). He cites library services like reference assistance, Internet access, story times, and author visits, as well as loans of other materials, though he says that with the exceptions of tools and people (and presumably other items like cake pans and ukuleles), lending will be effectively stopped by digitization as well. Libraries, Spalding adds, are "funded indirectly. Bookstores monetize their community value—whether it's an author reading or just the value of meeting cool people—by selling valuable objects. They create more value than they can realize. Public libraries, by contrast, monetize through government taxation, which is to say by periodically asking voters if they value them. As of now, despite some budgetary cuts, voters mostly do" (Spalding 2010).

So, libraries could end up being the keeper of the print flame, our buildings devoted less to books and more to community space, which may or may not fulfill everyone's vision of a library. Those intangible things Spalding mentions—the help from librarians, the literacy building, the programs—are all things libraries have now, and we're still struggling for funding most of the time. Better proactive advocacy can help. Debbie Herman, past president of the Connecticut Library Association, notes that libraries are often fantastic at pulling together support in a crisis, but not always as good at sustaining their efforts when the crisis had passed. Getting funding for a library in an eBook world will likely mean that not all libraries survive. Just as candle making was once handled by every household in New England and is now done largely in Deerfield, Massachusetts, by Yankee Candle, libraries will be fewer and farther between. Those that remain will likely be systems that serve larger populations or libraries that have made themselves indispensable to their communities (like Neiburger's own Ann Arbor has done).

This is perhaps a depressing scenario for librarians to contemplate, although many libraries have been moving from book temple to community space for years, so we may collectively be better off than we think. Print hasn't become quaint and atmospheric just yet, and the same economic hard times that have led to our own budget woes have also provided libraries with an opportunity to shine in their communities. eBooks may eventually make print books a specialty housed only at the few remaining bookstores and libraries, but in the interim, libraries have a chance to evolve and reinvent themselves for an eBook era.

A FEW FINAL THOUGHTS

At the 2012 Connecticut Library Association conference, I was on a panel about eBooks, moderated by ALA president Molly Raphael. The other panelists were an author, a publisher, and a bookseller. We discussed the current state of affairs with regard to eBooks and our collective uncertainty about the future. Afterward, a colleague came up to me and said he was frustrated because it seems like everyone keeps saying we have to wait and see how things will turn out and there aren't any solid answers yet. All I could tell him was that I knew exactly what he meant. eBooks are a frustrating topic because they're changing constantly, and yet there's never any resolution to the problems libraries have. I have felt this frustration acutely over the past several months. The best advice I have for my fellow librarians is to keep up with the changes as best you can (read widely, without taking anyone's opinion as gospel), and at some point, a Zen-like state vaguely resembling patience kicks in (at least some of the time). Some of that calm is predicated on being an observer, watching the eBook future unfold around you, which is not always satisfactory when librarians are feeling like libraries are the collateral damage of this disruptive moment in publishing and bookselling.

I hope this book has been useful to you. It's not meant to provide answers, but resources and points for discussion. Like everyone else who writes about libraries and eBooks, I want to say that libraries should demand a seat at the table to determine our own eBook future. But the process of writing this has taught me that there really isn't a table. Everyone is waiting for things to shake out, and snarling about their own place at the mythic table. Forces beyond our control, like the DOJ lawsuit, consumer preferences, and eReader innovations, will be powerful factors in the coming years. Our frustration will not bring any changes to bear on the eBook market.

However, that's not to say we don't have any power. Our greatest strength lies in our connection to our community. Publishers envy our relationships with readers, and I'd bet that even Amazon would love to have the insight into the consumer mind your typical reader's advisor does. Libraries like Ann Arbor's and Douglas County's use their place in the community to innovate and to connect. As Michael Porter says, libraries are content plus community. eBooks may be making us feel out of control and desperate when it comes to content, but if we keep turning our attention to our communities, we may find the solace and support we need to continue to build strong institutions that serve their patrons well and are well loved in return.

WORKS CITED

"About the Internet Archive." Internet Archive. http://www.archive.org/about/about.php (accessed November 13, 2011).

"About Mobipocket." Mobipocket. http://www.mobipocket.com/en/Corporate/AboutMobipocket.asp?Language=EN (accessed January 27, 2012).

"About eBook Library." EBL http://www.eblib.com/?p=about (accessed September 25, 2012).

"About Us." Random House website. http://www.randomhouse.com/about/history.html (accessed December 11, 2011).

"A Brief History of Copyright and Innovation." Teaching Copyright. http://www.teachingcopyright.org/curriculum/hs/2 (accessed January 28, 2012).

Agger, Michael. "The Internet Diet." Slate, June 7, 2012. http://www.slate.com/articles/arts/books/2010/06/the_internet_diet.single.html (last accessed September 25, 2012).

Albanese, Andrew. "ALA Midwinter 2012: Panel Tells Librarians to Go Forth and Digitize." *Publishers Weekly*. January 23, 2012a. http://www.publishersweekly.com/pw/by-topic/digital/copyright/article/50320-ala-midwinter-2012-panel-tells-librarians-to-go-forth-and-digitize.html (accessed February 5, 2012).

Albanese, Andrew. "Authors Guild Sues Libraries over Scan Plan." *Publishers Weekly*, September 13, 2011. http://www.publishersweekly.com/pw/by-topic/digital/copyright/article/48659-authors-guild-sues-libraries-over-scan-plan.html (accessed February 5, 2012).

Albanese, Andrew. "Fair Trade: Random House Will Raise Library E-book Prices but Commits to E-book Lending." *Publishers Weekly*, February 2, 2012b. http://www.publishersweekly.com/pw/by-topic/digital/content-and-e-books/article/50478-fair-trade-random-house-will-raise-library-e-book-prices-but-commits-to-e-book-lending.html (accessed February 5, 2012).

Albanese, Andrew. "Macmillan Poised to Test Library E-book Model." *Publishers Weekly*, September 24, 2012c. http://www.publishersweekly.com/pw/by -topic/digital/content-and-e-books/article/54083-macmillan-poised-to-test -library-e-book-model-.html (accessed September 24, 2012).

Albanese, Andrew. "OUP, Library Groups Strike Innovative Print/Digital Deal." *Publishers Weekly*, September 25, 2012d. http://www.publishersweekly. com/pw/by-topic/digital/content-and-e-books/article/54096-oup-library-groups -strike-innovative-print-digital-deal-.html (accessed September 25, 2012).

"Amazon's New Kindle Will Have Thin Profit Margin." NPR September 6, 2012. http://www.npr.org/2012/09/06/160697501/new-amazon-kindle-wont-yield -much-profit (accessed September 26, 2012).

Anderson, Nate. "Hands-On: Checking Out Library Books with Kindle Clunky, but Awesome." *arstechnica*, October 10, 2011. http://arstechnica.com/tech -policy/news/2011/10/hands-on-checking-out-library-books-with-kindle.ars (accessed December 27, 2011).

Anstice, Ian. "Zadie Smith." *Public Library News*, March 20, 2011. http://www .publiclibrariesnews.com/2011/03/changes-leicestershire-40-budget-4m-cut .html (accessed May 28, 2012).

Anyangwe, Eliza. "Talk Point: What Will the Impact of Apple's iBooks 2 Be on Education?" *Learning and Teaching Hub* (blog). *Guardian*, January 26, 2012. http://www.guardian.co.uk/higher-education-network/blog/2012/jan/26/ apple-ibooks-2-reinvent-textbooks (accessed September 25, 2012).

"Authors Guild Sues HathiTrust and 5 Universities Over Digitized Books." *The Ticker* (blog). *The Chronicle of Higher Education*, September 12, 2011. http://chronicle.com/blogs/ticker/authors-guild-sues-hathitrust-5-universities- over-digitized-books/36178 (accessed February 5, 2012).

"Background." World Intellectual Property Association TIGAR Project. http://www .visionip.org/tigar/en/background.html Accessed February 4, 2012.

Baddeley, Anna. "Ebooks: Winners in the Generation Game." *Guardian*, May 26, 2012. http://www.guardian.co.uk/books/2012/may/27/ebooks-growth-older -age-groups (accessed May 28, 2012).

Bane, Katie. "3M Cloud Library eBook Lending Service." *American Libraries*, May 14, 2012. http://americanlibrariesmagazine.org/solutions-and-services/ 3m-cloud-library-ebook-lending-service (accessed May 27, 2012).

Barrett, Brian. "You Can't Afford Apple's Education Revolution." Gizmodo, January 19, 2012. http://gizmodo.com/5877574/you-cant-afford-apples -education-revolution (accessed February 5, 2012).

Battles, Matthew. *Library: An Unquiet History*. New York: Norton, 2003.

Bell, Vaughn. "Don't Touch That Dial!" *Slate*, February 15, 2010. http://www.slate .com/articles/health_and_science/science/2010/02/dont_touch_that_dial.single .html (accessed September 25, 2012).

Berlucchi, Matteo. "More on DRM." *FutureBook*, January 29, 2012a. http://www .futurebook.net/content/more-drm (accessed January 30, 2012).

Berlucchi, Matteo. "Semi-random Thoughts on E-books, DRM & How to Increase Competition & Innovation in an Incumbent Dominated Market." Presentation at Digital Book World 2012. January 25, 2012b. http://prezi.com/2-jbb -klkdqw/dbw12/ (accessed January 27, 2012).

Berube, Rachel. "A 'License to Read': The Effect of E-Books on Publishers, Libraries, and the First Sale Doctrine." Selected Works of Rachel A. Berube. 2011 (accessed September 20, 2012).

Biba, Paul. "Kobo Has 10x Increase in Readers over Holidays; Top Ebooks by Country." TeleRead. January 5, 2012. http://www.teleread.com/paul-biba/kobo-has-10x-increase-in-readers-over-holidays-top-ebooks-by-country/ (accessed January 28, 2012).

Biggs, John. "Amazon Kindle HD Will Allow Users to Opt-out of 'Special Offers' for $15" TechCrunch, September 8, 2012. http://techcrunch.com/2012/09/08/amazon-kindle-hd-will-allow-users-to-opt-out-of-special-offers-for-15/ (accessed September 24, 2012).

Bjarnason, Baldur. "The iBook 2.0 Textbook Format." *Baldur Bjarnason*, January 19, 2012. http://www.baldurbjarnason.com/notes/the-ibooks-textbook-format/ (accessed January 27, 2012).

Blount, Roy, Jr. "The Kindle Swindle?" *New York Times*, February 24, 2009. http://www.nytimes.com/2009/02/25/opinion/25blount.html (accessed January 14, 2012).

Bolton, Nick. "Do E-readers Cause Eye Strain?" *Bits* (blog). *New York Times*, February 12, 2010. http://bits.blogs.nytimes.com/2010/02/12/do-e-readers-cause-eye-strain/ (accessed January, 28, 2012).

Bonfield, Brett. "The Ebook Cargo Cult." In the Library with the Lead Pipe. July 11, 2012. http://www.inthelibrarywiththeleadpipe.org/2012/the-ebook-cargo-cult/ (accessed July 12, 2012).

"Books in Browsers 2011: James Bridle, 'Books as Data.'" YouTube Video, 19:42. Posted by "OreillyMedia." October 31, 2011. http://www.youtube.com/watch?v=uTprAVmG204.

Booth, Char. "Unlocking HathiTrust: Inside the Librarians' Digital Library." *Library Journal*, June 9, 2011. http://www.libraryjournal.com/lj/communityacademiclibraries/890917-419/unlocking_hathitrust_inside_the_librarians.html.csp (accessed February 5, 2012).

Bosman, Julie. "Barnes & Noble Won't Sell Books from Amazon Publishing." *Media Decoder* (blog). *New York Times*, January 31, 2012a. http://mediadecoder.blogs.nytimes.com/2012/01/31/barnes-noble-says-it-wont-sell-books-published-by-amazon/ (accessed February 5, 2012).

Bosman, Julie. "The Bookstore's Last Stand." *New York Times*, January 28, 2012b. http://www.nytimes.com/2012/01/29/business/barnes-noble-taking-on-amazon-in-the-fight-of-its-life.html (accessed January 29, 2012).

Bosman, Julie. "E-readers Catch Younger Eyes and Go in Backpacks." *New York Times*, February 4, 2011. http://www.nytimes.com/2011/02/05/books/05ebooks.html?_r=1 (accessed December 28, 2011).

Bosman, Julie. "Judge Approves E-Book Pricing Settlement between Government and Publishers." *Media Decoder* (blog). *New York Times*, September 6, 2012c. http://mediadecoder.blogs.nytimes.com/2012/09/06/judge-approves-e-book-pricing-settlement-between-government-and-publishers/ (accessed September 24, 2012).

Bosman, Julie, and Matt Richtel. "Finding Your Book Interrupted ... by the Tablet You Read It On." *New York Times*, March 4, 2012. http://www.nytimes

.com/2012/03/05/business/media/e-books-on-tablets-fight-digital-distractions
.html (accessed May 19, 2012).

Bott, Ed. "How Apple Is Sabotaging an Open Standard for Digital Books." *The Ed Bott Report* (blog). *ZDNet*, January 22, 2012. http://www.zdnet.com/blog/ bott/how-apple-is-sabotaging-an-open-standard-for-digital-books/4378 (accessed January 27, 2012).

Brantley, Peter. "The Book and Its Discontents." Presentation at the Firebrand Community Conference, 2010. http://www.slideshare.net/naypinya/ reorganizing-the (accessed May 5, 2012).

Brantley, Peter. "Rich Books, Poor Society: Random House's Price Spike." *Publishers Weekly*, March 5, 2012. http://blogs.publishersweekly.com/blogs/ PWxyz/2012/03/05/rich-books-poor-society-random-houses-price-spike/ (accessed September 23, 2012).

Brantley, Peter. "What If the Future . . . (Is Like the Past)?" Presentation at the Presidio, November 2011. http://www.slideshare.net/naypinya/what-if-the -future-of-libraries (accessed December 28, 2011).

Bridle, James. "Bookcubes: Souvenirs of Digital Reading." *booktwo.org*, April 15, 2010a. http://booktwo.org/notebook/bookcubes/ (accessed May 19, 2012).

Bridle, James. "Walter Benjamin's Aura: Open Bookmarks and the Future Ebook." *booktwo.org*, October 5, 2010b. http://booktwo.org/notebook/open bookmarks/ (accessed May 19, 2012).

"A Brief History of Simon & Schuster." Simon & Schuster.biz. http://www .simonandschuster.biz/corporate/history (accessed December 11, 2011).

"British Kids Read Their eBooks on a Bigger Screen, Says New Study from Bowker." Bowker.co.uk, May 14, 2012. http://www.bowker.co.uk/en-UK/aboutus/ press_room/2012/pr_05142012.shtml (accessed September 24, 2012).

California Senate Bill No. 602. Title 1.81.15. Reader Privacy Act. October 2, 2011. http://www.leginfo.ca.gov/pub/11-12/bill/sen/sb_0601-0650/ (accessed May 5, 2012).

Carpenter, Todd. "Introduction to NISO Webinar on Ebook Preservation." NISO.org. May 23, 2012. http://www.niso.org/blog/?p=139 (accessed May 28, 2012).

Carr, Nicholas. "Books That Are Never Done Being Written." *Wall Street Journal*, December 31, 2011. http://online.wsj.com/article/SB100014240529 70203893404577098343417771160.html (accessed May 19, 2012).

Carr, Paul. "Book Piracy: A Non-issue." *TechCrunch*, August 23, 2011. http:// techcrunch.com/2011/08/23/book-piracy-a-non-issue/ (accessed May 5, 2012).

Chin, Robin. "The Codex Book." Transliteracies Project. January 30, 2006. http:// transliteracies.english.ucsb.edu/post/research-project/research-clearinghouse -individual/research-reports/the-codex-book (accessed May 19, 2012).

CIPA Bookshelf. "Update on CIPA/Douglas County Libraries e-Book Partnership." July 12, 2011. http://booksatcipa.wordpress.com/2011/07/12/update-on -cipadouglas-county-libraries-e-book-partnership/ (accessed December 28, 2011).

Circle, Alison. "The Ebook Evolution: How They'll Change Public Libraries." Presentation at the *Library Journal* Ebook Summit 2011, "Ebooks: The New Normal." October 12, 2011.

"Company" ebrary. http://www.ebrary.com/corp/company.jsp (accessed September 25, 2012).

"Company History." Hachette Book Group. http://www.hachettebookgroup.com/about_company-history.aspx (accessed December 11, 2011).

"Company Profile." HarperCollins website. http://harpercollins.com/footer/companyProfile.aspx (accessed December 11, 2011).

ComScore. "Smartphones and Tablets Drive Nearly 7 Percent of Total U.S. Digital Traffic." October 10, 2011. http://www.comscore.com/Press_Events/Press _Releases/2011/10/Smartphones_and_Tablets_Drive_Nearly_7_Percent_of _Total_U.S._Digital_Traffic (accessed November 25, 2011).

"Copyright." HathiTrust. http://www.hathitrust.org/copyright (accessed February 5, 2012).

Copyright and Digital Files. U.S. Copyright Office. http://www.copyright.gov/help/faq/faq-digital.html (accessed September 20, 2012).

"Copyright in the Library. Making Copies: Interlibrary Loan." Copyright Crash Course. http://copyright.lib.utexas.edu/l-108g.html (accessed January 28, 2012).

"DAISY Demystified." DAISYpedia. http://www.daisy.org/daisypedia/daisy -demystified (accessed February 5, 2012).

Dell'Antonia, K. J. "Why Books Are Better than e-Books for Children." *Motherlode* (blog). *New York Times*, December 28, 2011. http://parenting.blogs.nytimes .com/2011/12/28/why-books-are-better-than-e-books-for-children/?smid=tw -NYTMotherlode&seid=auto (accessed December 28, 2011).

"Digital Public Library of America: Pro and Con." *The Digital Shift*, October 13, 2011. http://www.thedigitalshift.com/2011/10/ebooks/digital-public-library -of-america-pro-and-con/ (accessed February 5, 2012).

"Digital Public Library of America Steering Committee Announces 'Beta Sprint.'" Berkman Center for Internet & Society. May 20, 2011. http://cyber.law .harvard.edu/newsroom/Digital_Public_Library_America_Beta_Sprint (accessed February 5, 2012).

Dilworth, Dianna. "74% of Book Buyers Have Never Bought an eBook." *eBook-Newser* (now *AppNewser*) (blog). *MediaBistro*, January 24, 2012. http:// www.mediabistro.com/ebooknewser/74-of-book-buyers-have-never-bought -an-ebook_b19645 (accessed January 28, 2012).

Doctorow, Cory. *Content: Selected Essays on Technology, Creativity, Copyright, and the Future of the Future.* San Francisco: Tachyon, 2008.

Doctorow, Cory. "Lockdown: The Coming War on General-Purpose Computing." *Boing Boing*, January 10, 2012a. http://boingboing.net/2012/01/10/lockdown.html (accessed January 27, 2012).

Doctorow, Cory. "National Federation for the Blind Protest at Authors Guild in NYC Today over Kindle Text-to-Speech." *Boing Boing*, April 6, 2009. http://boingboing.net/2009/04/06/national-federation.html (accessed January 14, 2012).

Doctorow, Cory. "Raising Money to Free Classic Volume on Africa's Oral History." *Boing Boing*, May 18, 2012b. http://boingboing.net/2012/05/18/raising -money-to-free-classic.html (accessed May 28, 2012).

Doctorow, Cory. "Sony Anti-customer Technology Roundup and Time-Line." *Boing Boing*, November 14, 2005. http://boingboing.net/2005/11/14/sony -anticustomer-te.html (accessed January 27, 2012).

Doctorow, Cory. "Why the Death of DRM Would Be Good News for Readers, Writers, and Publishers." *Guardian*, May 3, 2012c. http://www.guardian.co.uk/ technology/2012/may/03/death-of-drm-good-news (accessed May 12, 2012).

Duranceau, Ellen. "MIT Faculty Boycott Elsevier Journals." *MIT Libraries News*, January 27, 2012. http://libraries.mit.edu/sites/news/faculty-boycott-elsevier/ 7564/ (accessed February 5, 2012).

"E-Book Consumers Say 'Yes' to Tablets, Says BISG Study." Bowker. http://www .bowker.com/en-US/aboutus/press_room/2012/pr_04302012.shtml (accessed May 27, 2012).

"eBook FAQs." FollettShelf. http://www.aboutfollettebooks.com/ebooks-faq.cfm (accessed December 28, 2011).

"eBook formats." eBook Architects. http://ebookarchitects.com/conversions/ formats.php (accessed January 28, 2012).

"Elements of the DPLA." DPLA website. http://blogs.law.harvard.edu/dplaalpha/ about/elements-of-the-dpla/ (accessed February 5, 2012).

Elgan, Mike. "Why the Emotional Criticism of iBooks Author Is Wrong." *Cult of Mac*, January 21, 2012. http://www.cultofmac.com/141832/why-the -emotional-criticism-of-ibooks-author-is-wrong/ (accessed January 29, 2012).

Engleman, Eric. "Disability Groups Demand Full Return of Kindle Text-to-Speech." *Amazon Blog* (blog). *Tech Flash*, March 20, 2009. http://www.techflash.com/ seattle/2009/03/Disability_groups_demand_full_return_of_Kindles_text-to -speech_41583262.html (accessed February 4, 2012).

Enis, Matt. "Ebook Crowdfunding Platform Unglue.it Launched." *The Digital Shift*, May 17, 2012a. http://www.thedigitalshift.com/2012/05/ebooks/ebook -crowdfunding-platform-unglue-it-launched/ (accessed May 28, 2012).

Enis, Matt. "Momentum Builds for DCL's eBook Model." *The Digital Shift*, May 9, 2012b. http://www.thedigitalshift.com/2012/05/ebooks/momentum-builds -for-dcls-ebook-model/ (accessed May 28, 2012).

Enis, Matt. "To Remain Relevant, Libraries Should Help Patrons Create." *The Digital Shift*, May 25, 2012c. http://www.thedigitalshift.com/2012/05/ux/to -remain-relevant-libraries-should-help-patrons-create/ (accessed May 28, 2012).

"Entire eBook Catalogs to Be Available for Discovery, Sampling & Links to Booksellers ... from the Public Library." OverDrive. Press release, October 10, 2011. http://overdrive.com/News/Entire-eBook-Catalogs-to-be-Available -for-Discovery-Sampling—Links-to-BooksellersFrom-the-Public-Library (accessed November 26, 2011).

Espositio, Joseph. "A Dialogue on Patron-Driven Acquisitions." *The Scholarly Kitchen*, January 3, 2012. http://scholarlykitchen.sspnet.org/2012/01/03/ a-dialogue-on-patron-driven-acquisitions/ (accessed January 26, 2012).

EurekaAlert. "Plugged into Learning: Computers Help Students Achieve." January 16, 2012. http://www.eurekalert.org/pub_releases/2012-01/ cu-pil011612.php (accessed May 28, 2012).

"Fair Use." Copyright & Fair Use Stanford University Libraries. http://fairuse .stanford.edu/Copyright_and_Fair_Use_Overview/chapter9/index.html (accessed September 20, 2012).

"Fair Use Frequently Asked Questions." Teaching Copyright. http://www
.teachingcopyright.org/handout/fair-use-faq (accessed January 28, 2012).

"Fair Use Frequently Asked Questions (and Answers)." Electronic Frontier
Foundation. http://w2.eff.org/IP/eff_fair_use_faq.php (accessed January 28,
2012).

"FAQ." CLOCKSS. http://www.clockss.org/clockss/FAQ (accessed May 28, 2012).

"FAQ." FollettShelf. http://www.aboutfollettebooks.com/all-faqs.cfm#javascript:
(accessed September 24, 2012).

"FAQ." Freading. http://freading.com/questions/index (accessed September 25,
2012).

Ferguson, Joey. "S.L. Library Pays More for Ebooks than for Print." *Deseret News*,
November 18, 2011. http://www.deseretnews.com/article/705394575/SL
-library-pays-more-for-e-books-than-for-print.html. (accessed December 14,
2011).

Fister, Barbara. "LJ Talks to David Weinberger about the Living Web." *Library
Journal*, May 22, 2012. http://lj.libraryjournal.com/2012/05/future-of
-libraries/questions-for-david-weinberger/ (accessed May 28, 2012).

Fister, Barbara. "Occupy Knowledge: It's Ours, After All." *Library Babel Fish*
(blog). Inside Higher Ed, October 20, 2011. http://www.insidehighered.com/
blogs/occupy-knowledge-its-ours-after-all (accessed May 19, 2012).

Fister, Barbara. "Puzzled by Patron-Driven Acquisitions." *Library Babel Fish* (blog).
Inside Higher Ed, November 11, 2010. http://www.insidehighered.com/
blogs/library_babel_fish/puzzled_by_patron_driven_acquisitions (accessed
January 26, 2012).

Fleishhacker, Joy. "Transmedia Trailblazers: SLJ Reviews Six Multiplatform Titles."
The Digital Shift, November 16, 2011. http://www.thedigitalshift.com/2011/
11/ebooks/transmedia-trailblazers-slj-reviews-six-multiplatform-titles/
(accessed November 26, 2011).

Foresman, Chris. "DOJ, State AGs Also Investigating Possible e-Book Collusion."
arstechnica, December 7, 2011. http://arstechnica.com/tech-policy/news/
2011/12/doj-state-ags-also-investigating-possible-e-book-collusion.ars
(accessed February 5, 2012).

"Freading" Library Ideas http://www.libraryideas.com/freading.html (accessed
September 24, 2012).

Fried, Ian. "Apple's iPod Spurs Mixed Reactions." *CNET*, October 23, 2001. http://
news.cnet.com/Apples-iPod-spurs-mixed-reactions/2100-1040_3-274821.
html (accessed January 28, 2012).

Gallagher, David F. "For the Mix Tape, a Digital Upgrade and Notoriety." *New
York Times*, January 30, 2003. http://www.nytimes.com/2003/01/30/
technology/for-the-mix-tape-a-digital-upgrade-and-notoriety.html?src=pm
(accessed January 28, 2012).

Geere, Duncan. "DRM Serves as Piracy Incentive, Study Finds." *Wired.co.uk*,
October 10, 2011. http://www.wired.co.uk/news/archive/2011-10/10/drm
-piracy-incentive (accessed January 27, 2012).

Gilmor, Dan. "The Great Ebook Price Swindle." *Guardian*, December 23, 2011.
http://www.guardian.co.uk/commentisfree/cifamerica/2011/dec/23/ebook-price
-swindle-publishing (accessed February 5, 2012).

Glazman, Daniel. "iBooks Author, a Nice Tool, But. . . . " *Glazblog*, January 20, 2012. http://www.glazman.org/weblog/dotclear/index.php?post/2012/01/20/ iBooks-Author-a-nice-tool-but (accessed January 27, 2012).

Goerner, Phil. "Making the Shift: A School Librarian Considers the Douglas County Ebook Model." *The Digital Shift*, May 2, 2012. http://www.thedigitalshift .com/2012/05/ebooks/making-the-shift-a-school-librarian-considers-the-douglas -county-ebook-model/ (accessed May 28, 2012).

Goldberg, Beverly. "Two Colorado Libraries Break New E-Book Ground." *American Libraries*, March 16, 2011. http://americanlibrariesmagazine.org/ news/03162011/two-colorado-libraries-break-new-e-book-ground (accessed December 28, 2011).

Grames, Juliet. Interview by author. Phone call, May 14, 2012.

Grandinetti, Russ. "A Kindle New Year: Looking Back and Looking Forward." Digital Book World Conference. Sheraton Hotel & Towers. New York, January 25, 2012.

Green, Sarah. "Amazon Should Partner with Independent Bookstores." *Harvard Business Review Blog Network*, December 27, 2011. http://blogs.hbr.org/ hbr/hbreditors/2011/12/amazon_should_partner_with_ind.html (accessed January 2, 2012).

Greenfield, Jeremy. "Are Children's E-books Really Terrible for Your Children?" *Digital Book World*, November 21, 2011a. http://www.digitalbookworld .com/2011/are-childrens-e-books-really-terrible-for-your-children/ (accessed November 26, 2011).

Greenfield, Jeremy. "For Reading and Learning, Kids Prefer E-books to Print Books." *Digital Book World*, January 9, 2012. http://www.digitalbookworld .com/2012/for-reading-and-learning-kids-prefer-e-books-to-print-books/ (accessed February 4, 2012).

Greenfield, Jeremy. "Ten Bold Predictions for Book Publishing in 2012." *Digital Book World*, December 19, 2011b. http://www.digitalbookworld.com/ 2011/ten-bold-predictions-for-book-publishing-in-2012/ (accessed January 2, 2012).

Griffey, Jason. "eBooks, Filetype, and DRM." *Pattern Recognition*, August 25, 2010. http://jasongriffey.net/wp/2010/08/25/ebooks-filetype-and-drm/ (accessed January 27, 2012).

Guernsey, Lisa. "Are Ebooks Any Good?" *School Library Journal*, June 1, 2011. http://www.schoollibraryjournal.com/slj/printissuecurrentissue/890540-427/ are_ebooks_any_good.html.csp (accessed February 5, 2012).

Hadro, Josh, and Francine Fialkoff. "HarperCollins, OverDrive Respond as 26 Loan Cap on Ebook Debate Heats Up." *Library Journal*, March 1, 2011. http:// www.libraryjournal.com/lj/home/889500-264/harpercollins_overdrive_respond _as_26.html.csp (accessed December 14, 2011).

Hamaker, Charles. "Ebooks on Fire: Controversies Surrounding Ebooks in Libraries." *Searcher Magazine* 19, no. 10 (December 2011). http://www .infotoday.com/searcher/dec11/Hamaker.shtml (accessed December 4, 2011).

Hambien, Matt. "Kobo Announces $149 E-reader to be Sold by Borders." *ComputerWorld*, March 25, 2010. http://www.computerworld.com/s/article/ 9174123/Kobo_announces_149_e_reader_to_be_sold_by_Borders_?taxonomy Id=140 (accessed January 28, 2012).

Hamilton, Buffy. "Next Steps in the eReader Journey: The Nook Simple Touch." *The Unquiet Librarian*, August 11, 2011a. http://theunquietlibrarian .wordpress.com/2011/08/11/next-steps-in-the-ereader-journey-the-nook-simple -touch/ (accessed December 28, 2011).

Hamilton, Buffy. "Why We Won't Purchase More Kindles at the Unquiet Library." *The Unquiet Librarian*, July 27, 2011b. http://theunquietlibrarian.word press.com/2011/07/27/why-we-wont-purchase-more-kindles-at-the-unquiet -library/ (accessed December 28, 2011).

Harris, Christopher. "Ebooks and School Libraries." *American Libraries*, January 13, 2012a. http://americanlibrariesmagazine.org/features/01132012/ ebooks-and-school-libraries?utm_source=dlvr.it&utm_medium=twitter&utm _campaign=amlibraries (accessed February 5, 2012).

Harris, Christopher. "Has Hachette Forgotten How to Publish?" American Libraries, September 13, 2012b. http://www.americanlibrariesmagazine.org/e-content/ has-hachette-forgotten-how-publish (accessed September 23, 2012).

Harris, Christopher. "LJ/SLJ Ebook Summit 2011: 'Don't Buy Ebooks.'" *The Digital Shift*, October 7, 2011. http://www.thedigitalshift.com/2011/10/ebooks/ ebook-summit-2011-dont-buy-ebooks/ (accessed December 27, 2011).

Hastings, Jeffery. "Test Drive." *School Library Journal*, May 1, 2012. http://www .schoollibraryjournal.com/slj/articles/atechnology/894174-464/test_drive.html .csp (accessed May 28, 2012).

"HathiTrust Answers Authors Guild Lawsuit; Trial Date Set." *Publishers Weekly*, December 5, 2011. http://www.publishersweekly.com/pw/by-topic/digital/ copyright/article/49742-hathitrust-answers-authors-guild-lawsuit-trial-schedule -set.html (accessed February 5, 2012).

Head, Alison J., and Michael B. Eisenberg. *Truth Be Told: How College Students Evaluate and Use Information in the Digital Age*. Washington, DC: The Information School, 2010. http://projectinfolit.org/pdfs/PIL_Fall2010 _Survey_FullReport1.pdf (accessed January 26, 2012).

Hellman, Eric. "Attributor Ebook Piracy Numbers Don't Add Up." *Go to Hellman*, October 20, 2010a. http://go-to-hellman.blogspot.com/2010/10/attributor- ebook-piracy-numbers-dont.html (accessed February 5, 2012).

Hellman, Eric. "Consumer Interest in Pirated eBooks Is Even Lower than I Thought." Go to Hellman, November 6, 2010b. http://go-to-hellman.blog spot.com/2010/11/consumer-interest-in-pirated-ebooks-is.html (accessed September 24, 2012)

Hellman, Eric. "It's Not about Libraries, It's about Amazon." *Go to Hellman*, November 25, 2011a. http://go-to-hellman.blogspot.com/2011/11/its-not -about-libraries-its-about.html (accessed December 31, 2011).

Hellman, E. S. "Open Access E-books." In *The No Shelf Required Guide to E-book Purchasing*, edited by Sue Polanka. *Library Technology Reports* 47, no. 8 (November/December 2011b): chap. 4.

Hellman, Eric. "Why I'm Not Mad at Amazon." *Go to Hellman*, August 10, 2012. http://go-to-hellman.blogspot.com/2012/08/why-im-not-mad-at-amazon.html (accessed September 24, 2012).

Hellman, Eric. "Why ProQuest Bought Ebrary." *Go to Hellman*, January 15, 2011c. http://go-to-hellman.blogspot.com/2011/01/why-proquest-bought-ebrary.html (accessed May 23, 2012).

Hill, Nate. "An eBook Is Not a Book." *The PLA Blog*, January 8, 2012. http://plablog.org/2012/01/an-ebook-is-not-a-book.html (accessed May 19, 2012).

Hinken, Susan, and Emily McElroy. "Consortial Purchasing of E-Books." In *The No Shelf Required Guide to E-book Purchasing*, edited by Sue Polanka. *Library Technology Reports* 47, no. 8 (November/December 2011): chap. 2.

"History." Penguin website. http://us.penguingroup.com/static/pages/aboutus/history.html (accessed December 11, 2011).

Hoffelder, Nate. "RIP: Mobipocket 2000–2011." *The Digital Reader*, November 2, 2011. http://www.the-digital-reader.com/2011/11/02/rip-mobipocket-2000-2011/ (accessed September 19, 2012)

Houghton, Sarah. "Libraries Got Screwed by Amazon and Overdrive." *Librarian in Black*, October 18, 2011a. http://librarianinblack.net/librarianinblack/2011/10/wegotscrewed.html (accessed December 27, 2011).

Houghton, Sarah. "Open Library Offers Libraries a Third Choice for Ebooks." *Librarian in Black*, July 5, 2011b. http://librarianinblack.net/librarianinblack/2011/07/open-library-offers-libraries-a-third-choice-for-ebooks.html (accessed February 5, 2012).

Hsu, Michael. "Read Me an E-Book Story?" *Wall Street Journal*, November 19, 2011. http://online.wsj.com/article/SB10001424052970204190504577040443832284170.html?mod=WSJ_article_comments#articleTabs=article (accessed December 28, 2011).

"Information about the Authors Guild Lawsuit." HathiTrust. http://www.hathitrust.org/authors_guild_lawsuit_information (accessed February 5, 2012).

Ingram, Matthew. "Do We Want Textbooks to Live in Apple's Walled Garden?" *Gigaom*, January 19, 2012. http://gigaom.com/2012/01/19/do-we-want-textbooks-to-live-in-apples-walled-garden/ (accessed February 5, 2012).

International Digital Publishing Forum. "Epub." 2012. http://idpf.org/epub (accessed January 27, 2012).

International Digital Publishing Forum. "Epub 3 Overview." October 11, 2011. http://idpf.org/epub/30/spec/epub30-overview.html (accessed January 27, 2012).

Jackson, Lesley W. "Netlibrary." *Journal of the Medical Library Association* 92, no. 2 (April 2004): 284–85. http://www.ncbi.nlm.nih.gov/pmc/articles/PMC385321/ (accessed December 18, 2011).

James, Lori. "What Publishing Can Learn From the Romance Genre." Digital Book World Conference. Sheraton Hotel & Towers. New York, January 24, 2012.

Jarrard, Kyle. "Where Do e-Books Go When You Do?" *New York Times*, May 10, 2012. http://www.nytimes.com/2012/05/11/opinion/where-do-e-books-go-when-you-do.html (accessed May 28, 2012).

Jarvis, Jeff. "Network Knowledge." Buzz Machine. January 16, 2012. http://buzzmachine.com/2012/01/16/network-knowledge/ (accessed January 28, 2012).

"Justice Department Reaches Three Settlements under the Americans with Disabilities Act Regarding the Use of Electronic Book Readers." Department of Justice website. January 13, 2010. http://www.justice.gov/opa/pr/2010/January/10-crt-030.html (accessed February 4, 2012).

Kalder, Daniel. "E-Elmo: How Sesame Street Is Adapting to Digital." Publishing Perspectives. November 18, 2011. http://publishingperspectives.com/2011/11/e-elmo-sesame-street-adapting-digital/ (accessed November 26, 2011).

Katz, Amanda. "How We Read Now." *Boston.com*, July 17, 2011. http://articles
.boston.com/2011-07-17/yourtown/29784807_1_e-books-book-sales-e-reader/
4 (accessed January 28, 2012).

Kearney, A. T., and Bookrepublic. "Do Readers Dream of Electronic Books?" Presentation at the Publisher's Launch conference, October 10, 2011. http://
www.ifbookthen.com/wp-content/uploads/2011/10/research.pdf (accessed
January 28, 2012).

Keir, Thomas. "E-book Piracy Is Here. So What?" *PC World*, November 29, 2010.
http://www.pcworld.com/businesscenter/article/211941/ebook_piracy_is_here
_so_what.html (accessed January 8, 2012).

Kelley, Michael. "All 50 State Librarians Vote to Form Alliance with Internet
Archive's Open Library." *The Digital Shift*, November 4, 2011a. http://www
.thedigitalshift.com/2011/11/ebooks/all-50-state-librarians-vote-to-form-alliance
-with-internet-archives-open-library/ (accessed November 13, 2011).

Kelley, Michael. "Amazon's Lending Library Now Holds over 66,000 Ebooks." *The
Digital Shift*, December 28, 2011b. http://www.thedigitalshift.com/2011/12/
ebooks/amazons-library-lending-now-holds-over-65000-ebooks/ (accessed
December 30, 2011).

Kelley, Michael. "Consortium of 25 Libraries in Connecticut Votes to Boycott
Random House." *The Digital Shift*, April 5, 2012a. http://www.thedigital
shift.com/2012/04/ebooks/consortium-of-25-libraries-in-connecticut-votes-to
-boycott-random-house/ (accessed May 18, 2012).

Kelley, Michael. "Ebrary Cultivates a Niche in the Public Library Market." *The Digital Shift*. May 22, 2012b. http://www.thedigitalshift.com/2012/05/ebooks/
ebrary-cultivates-a-niche-in-the-public-library-market/ (accessed May 28,
2012).

Kelley, Michael. "EBSOC Previews Remodeled Platform Integrating NetLibrary
Ebooks." *Library Journal*, March 23, 2011c. http://www.libraryjournal
.com/lj/newslettersnewsletterbucketacademicnewswire/889816-440/ebsco
_previews_remodeled_platform_integrating.html.csp (accessed December 18,
2011).

Kelley, Michael. "Hachette Taking a Close Look at Risks and Benefits of Library
Ebook Lending." *Library Journal*, August 23, 2011d. http://www.library
journal.com/lj/home/891756-264/hachette_taking_a_close_look.html.csp
(accessed January 29, 2012).

Kelley, Michael. "HathiTrust Collection Surpasses 10 Million Volumes." *The
Digital Shift*, January 16, 2012c. http://www.thedigitalshift.com/2012/01/
digital-libraries/hathitrust-collection-surpasses-10-million-volumes/ (accessed
February 5, 2012).

Kelley, Michael. "Kansas State Librarian Can Transfer Thousands of Titles from
OverDrive to 3M at No Charge." *Library Journal*, October 10, 2011e.
http://www.libraryjournal.com/lj/home/892348-264/kansas_state_librarian
_can_transfer.html.csp (accessed May 12, 2012).

Kelley, Michael. "Librarians Face Patrons Unhappy with Penguin Policy Change;
ALA Condemns Ebook Decision." *The Digital Shift*, November 22, 2011f.
http://www.thedigitalshift.com/2011/11/ebooks/librarians-face-patrons-unhappy
-with-penguin-policy-change-ala-condemns-ebook-decision/ (accessed December 14, 2011).

Kelley, Michael. "Librarians Feel Sticker Shock as Price for Random House Ebooks Rises as Much as 300 Percent." *The Digital Shift*, March 2, 2012d.

Kelley, Michael. "Playing It Safe with Patron Confidentiality and Ebooks." *Library Journal*. April 25, 2011g. http://www.libraryjournal.com/lj/home/890319 -264/playing_it_safe_with_patron.html.csp (accessed January 30, 2012).

Kelley, Michael. "With Axis 360, Baker& Taylor Establishes a Foothold in the Ebook Distribution Market." *The Digital Shift*, March 7, 2012e. http://www .thedigitalshift.com/2012/03/ebooks/with-axis-360-baker-taylor-establishes-a -foothold-in-the-ebook-distribution-market/ (accessed May 22, 2012).

Kirchhoff, Amy. "E-book Preservation." In *No Shelf Required 2*, edited by Sue Polanka, 75–89. Chicago: American Library Association, 2012.

Konnikova, Maria. "How to Make a Book Disappear." *The Atlantic*, September 18, 2012. http://www.theatlantic.com/entertainment/archive/2012/09/how-to -make-a-book-disappear/262469/ (accessed September 25, 2012).

LaGarde, Jennifer, and Christine James. "E-reader Adoption in the School Library Media Center." In *No Shelf Required 2*, edited by Sue Polanka, 191–201. Chicago: American Library Association, 2012.

Landgraf, Greg. "How Kansas Owned Its Ebooks." *Inside Scoop* (blog). *American Libraries*, January 21, 2012. http://americanlibrariesmagazine.org/inside -scoop/how-kansas-owned-its-ebooks (accessed January 29, 2012).

LaRue, Jamie. Interview by the author. Email September 28, 2011–October 10, 2011.

"Law and Technology Timeline." Teaching Copyright. http://www.teaching copyright.org/download/handout/tc_law_and_technology_timeline.pdf (accessed January 28, 2012).

"Legal Issues." Digital Preservation Management. http://www.dpworkshop.org/ dpm-eng/challenges/accountability.html (accessed May 28, 2012).

Lehrer, Jonah. "Our Cluttered Minds." *New York Times*, June 3, 2010. http://www .nytimes.com/2010/06/06/books/review/Lehrer-t.html (accessed May 19, 2012).

Lessig, Lawrence. *Code Version 2.0*. New York: Basic Books, 2006.

Levine, Robert. *Free Ride: How Digital Parasites re Destroying the Culture Business, and How the Culture Business Can Fight Back*. New York: Doubleday, 2011.

Libraries Online, Inc. Press Release, April 6, 2012. http://www.lioninc.org/new/ lionincrandomhouse.pdf (accessed May 18, 2012).

"LJ Book Review Editor Heather McCormack to Manage 3M Ebook Lending Collection Development." *Library Journal*, July 12, 2012. http://lj.library journal.com/2012/07/people/lj-book-review-editor-to-manage-3m-collection -development/ (accessed September 23, 2012)

Litte, Jane. "DOJ Lawsuit Update: Where Windowing Becomes Important." *Dear Author*, May 16, 2012. http://dearauthor.com/features/industry-news/ doj-lawsuit-update-where-windowing-becomes-important/ (accessed May 18, 2012).

"Macmillan: A Short History." Macmillan website http://us.macmillan.com/splash/ about/history.html (accessed September 23, 2012).

Maier, Rob. "Libraries Own Random House Ebooks." *E-Content* (blog). *American Libraries*, May 10, 2012. http://americanlibrariesmagazine.org/e-content/ libraries-own-random-house-ebooks (accessed May 12, 2012).

Manjoo, Farhad. "Don't Support Your Local Bookseller." *Slate*, December 13, 2011. http://www.slate.com/articles/technology/technology/2011/12/ independent_bookstores_vs_amazon_buying_books_online_is_better_for_authors _better_for_the_economy_and_better_for_you_.html (accessed January 29, 2012).

Mason, Amy. "Mainstream Access to E-Books- What Works, What Doesn't, and What Is Still Unclear." *Braille Monitor*, January 2012. http://www.nfb.org/ images/nfb/publications/bm/bm12/bm1201/bm120105.htm (accessed May 22, 2012).

McCormack, Heather. "A Most Optimistic Unconference: Publishers, Libraries, and Independent Bookstores at Digital Book World 2012." *Library Journal*, January 29, 2012. http://reviews.libraryjournal.com/2012/01/in-the-bookroom/ publishing/a-most-optimistic-unconference-publishers-libraries-and-independent -bookstores-at-digital-book-world-2012/ (accessed January 29, 2012).

McGuire, Seanan. "Across the Digital Divide." *Rose-Owls and Pumpkin Girls*, September 16, 2011. http://seanan-mcguire.livejournal.com/390067.html (accessed May 28, 2012).

Messieh, Nancy. "Does E-book Piracy Really Matter?" *The Next Web*, June 24, 2011. http://thenextweb.com/media/2011/06/24/does-e-book-piracy-really -matter/ (accessed January 8, 2012).

Miller, Laura. "Can Bells and Whistles Save the Book?" *Salon*, February 1, 2012. http://www.salon.com/2012/02/02/can_bells_and_whistles_save_the_book/ singleton/ (accessed February 4, 2012).

Miller, Laura. " 'The Waste Land': T. S. Eliot Takes the App Store." *Salon*, June 15, 2011. http://www.salon.com/books/laura_miller/2011/06/14/the_waste_land (accessed January, 28, 2012).

Miller, Matthew. "Android Tablet Market Share Up 10%, iPad Down 10% through 2011." *The Mobile Gadgeteer* (blog). ZDNet, January 27, 2012. http://www .zdnet.com/blog/mobile-gadgeteer/android-tablet-market-share-up-10-ipad -down-10-through-2011/5430 (accessed January 28, 2012).

Mims, Christopher. "Will E-books Destroy the Democratizing Effects of Reading?" *Technology Review*, September 21, 2011. http://www.technologyreview .com/blog/mimssbits/27185/?p1=blogs (accessed May 28, 2012).

Mitchell, Dan. "Yes B&N, Cut the Nook Loose." *CNNMoney*, January 6, 2012. http://tech.fortune.cnn.com/2012/01/06/bn-cut-the-nook-loose/ (accessed January 29, 2012).

Morgan, Mary. "Ann Arbor Library Signs Digital Music Deal." *Ann Arbor Chronicle*, April 28, 2011. http://annarborchronicle.com/2011/04/28/ann -arbor-library-signs-digital-music-deal/ (accessed December 28, 2011).

Murray, Peter. "Just in Time Acquisitions versus Just in Case Acquisitions." *Disruptive Library Technology Jester*, August 2, 2006. http://dltj.org/article/just-in -time-versus-just-in-case-acquisitions/ (accessed September 26, 2012).

"MyiLibrary Demo." MyiLibrary website. http://www.myilibrary.com/Home.aspx. (accessed December 18, 2011).

National Endowment for the Arts. *To Read or Not to Read*. Research Report #47. Washington, DC: Office of Research and Analysis, 2007. http://www.nea .gov/research/toread.pdf (accessed November 26, 2011).

"National Federation of the Blind Assists in Litigation against Free Library of Philadelphia." National Federation of the Blind website. May 2, 2012. http://nfb

.org/national-federation-blind-assists-litigation-against-philadelphia-free-library (accessed May 28, 2012).

Nawotka, Edward. "Is the Serendipity of Book Discovery Dead in the Age of E-books?" *Publishing Perspectives*, March 2, 2010. http://publishing perspectives.com/2010/03/is-the-serendipity-of-book-discovery-dead-in-the -age-of-e-books/ (accessed January 29, 2012).

Neiburger, Eli. "eBook Evolution: How They'll Change Public Libraries." Presentation at the *Library Journal* 2011a eBook summit, "Ebooks: The New Normal," October 12, 2011.

Neiburger, Eli. "eBooks and Libraries in This Century." Presentation at Connecticut Library Consortium's Trendspotting 2011, April 5, 2011b. http://www .ctlibrarians.org/displaycommon.cfm?an=1&subarticlenbr=36 (accessed September 25, 2012).

Neiburger, Eli. "Libraries Are Screwed." Presentation at the *Library Journal* eBook Summit, "Libraries at the Tipping Point," September 29, 2010. http://www .youtube.com/watch?v=KqAwj5ssU2c (accessed February 5, 2012).

Newman, Bobbi. "Should Libraries Get Out of the eBook Business?" Librarian By Day, March 7, 2012. http://librarianbyday.net/2012/03/07/should-libraries -get-out-of-the-ebook-business/ (accessed September 24, 2012).

"Newsmaker: Joanne Budler." *American Libraries*, January 3, 2012. http:// americanlibrariesmagazine.org/columns/newsmaker/joanne-budler (accessed January 29, 2012).

Oder, Norman. "Focusing on WorldCat, OCLC Sells NetLibrary to EBSCO, Thins FirstSearch." *Library Journal*, March 17, 2010. http://www.libraryjournal .com/lj/technologyproductsvendors/884426-296/focusing_on_worldcat_oclc _sells.html.csp (accessed December 18, 2011).

O'Leary, Brian. "The Opportunity in Abundance." Magellan Media, October 31, 2011. http://www.magellanmediapartners.com/index.php/mmcp/article/the _opportunity_in_abundance/ (accessed November 21, 2011).

"One in Six Americans Now Use E-reader with One in Six Likely to Purchase in the Next Six Months." Harris Interactive, September 19, 2011. http://www .harrisinteractive.com/NewsRoom/HarrisPolls/tabid/447/mid/1508/articleId/ 864/ctl/ReadCustom%20Default/Default.aspx (accessed January 28, 2012).

Orr, Cynthia. "Secrets of Ebook Success." *Library Journal*, September 15, 2011. http://www.libraryjournal.com/lj/community/managinglibraries/891747-273/ secrets_of_ebook_success_.html.csp (accessed February 5, 2012).

Ovide, Shira. "Microsoft Hooks onto Nook." *Wall Street Journal*, May 2, 2012. http://online.wsj.com/article/SB10001424052702303916904577375502392 129654.html (accessed May 27, 2012).

Owen, Laura Hazard. "Buy a 1-Year NYT Subscription, Get the Nook Free." *Paid-Content*, January 9, 2012a. http://paidcontent.org/article/419-buy-a-1-year -nook-nyt-subscription-get-the-nook-free/ (accessed January 28, 2012).

Owen, Laura Hazard. "Ebook Price Drops Begin—and Apple Is Discounting, Too." PaidContent, September 11, 2012d http://paidcontent.org/2012/09/11/ the-price-drops-begin-what-do-harpercollins-ebooks-cost-now/ (accessed September 24, 2012).

Owen, Laura Hazard. "What the DOJ E-book Lawsuit Means for Readers Now." *PaidContent*, April 16, 2012b. http://paidcontent.org/2012/04/16/what

-does-the-doj-e-book-pricing-lawsuit-mean-for-readers-now/ (accessed May 18, 2012).

Owen, Laura Hazard. "'Why I Break DRM on e-Books': A Publishing Exec Speaks Out." *PaidContent*, April 24, 2012c http://paidcontent.org/2012/04/24/ breaking-drm-publishing-exec/ (accessed September 20, 2012).

Parker, Kathy. "Using E-books with Reluctant Readers." In *No Shelf Required 2*, edited by Sue Polanka, 212–18. Chicago: American Library Association, 2012.

Patel, Nilay. "Sony Announces Reader Daily Edition, Free Library Ebook Check-outs." *Engadget*, August 25, 2009. http://www.engadget.com/2009/08/25/ sony-announces-daily-edition-reader/ (accessed January 2, 2012).

"Peanuts and Loud Crow Partner to Create Digital Book Apps." Loudcrow Interactive, November 17, 2011. http://loudcrow.com/peanuts-and-loud-crow -partner-to-create-digital-book-apps (accessed November 25, 2011).

Petri, Ken. "Accessibility Issues in E-books and E-book Readers." In *No Shelf Required 2*, edited by Sue Polanka, 45–66. Chicago: American Library Association, 2012.

Petrocelli, William. "Who's Snooping around Bookstores? Lots of People." *Huffington Post*, January 3, 2012. http://www.huffingtonpost.com/william -petrocelli/book-stores-ebooks_b_1179985.html (accessed January 30, 2012).

Phan, Tai, Laura Hardesty, Jamie Hug, and Cindy Sheckells. *Academic Libraries: 2010*. U.S. Department of Education. Washington, DC: National Center for Education Statistics, 2011. http://nces.ed.gov/pubs2012/2012365.pdf (accessed February 5, 2012).

Phaxia, Steve, and John Parsons. "Library Patrons and Ebook Usage." *Library Journal Patron Profiles* 1, no. 1 (October 2011): 1–38.

Pilkington, Mercy. "Kobo Announces the Launch of Its Own Publishing Platform." *Good Ereader*, October 27, 2011. http://goodereader.com/blog/electronic -readers/kobo-announces-the-launch-of-its-own-publishing-platform/ (accessed February 5, 2012).

Pinkowski, Jennifer. "Recorded Books, NetLibrary in Lawsuits over Audiobook Service." *Library Journal*, July 17, 2007. http://www.libraryjournal.com/article/ CA6460213.html (accessed December 18, 2011).

Plotz, John. "This Book Is 119 Years Overdue." *Slate*, November 17, 2011. http:// www.slate.com/articles/arts/culturebox/2011/11/the_wondrous_database_that _reveals_what_books_americans_checked_out_of_the_library_a_century_ago _.single.html (accessed December 4, 2011).

Poeter, Damon. "Report: Amazon to Sell $79 Kindles at a Loss." *PCMag*, November 10, 2011. http://www.pcmag.com/article2/0,2817,2396248,00.asp (accessed December 29, 2011).

Pogue, David. "Some Ebooks Are More Equal than Others." *Pogue's Posts* (blog). *New York Times*, July 17, 2009. http://pogue.blogs.nytimes.com/2009/07/ 17/some-e-books-are-more-equal-than-others/#?wtoeid=growl1_r1_v1 (accessed January 28, 2012).

Pogue, David. "Barnes & Noble's E-book Reader Glows in the Dark" *State of the Art* (blog). *New York Times*, April 24, 2012. http://www.nytimes.com/ 2012/04/26/technology/personaltech/barnes-nobles-e-book-reader-glows-in -the-dark.html?smid=pl-share (accessed September 19, 2012).

Porter, Michael. Interview by the author. Skype. November 9, 2011.

Porter, Michael. Interview by the author. Skype. May 2, 2012.

Porter, Michael, Matt Weaver, and Bobbi Newman. "E-book Sea Change in Public Libraries." In *No Shelf Required 2*, edited by Sue Polanka, 120–135. Chicago: American Library Association, 2012.

"Pre-Packaged Products." ebrary. http://www.ebrary.com/corp/products.jsp (accessed September 25, 2012).

Price, Gary. "eBooks, Privacy, and the Library." *Infodocket*, September 27, 2011. http://infodocket.com/2011/09/27/8350/ (accessed January 30, 2012).

Price, Gary, and Matt Enis. "ALA, LaRue Respond to Hachette Price Increase." *The Digital Shift*, September 14, 2012. http://www.thedigitalshift.com/2012/09/ebooks/ala-larue-respond-to-hachette-price-increase/ (accessed September 23, 2012)

Rainie, Lee. "Tablet and E-book Reader Ownership Nearly Double over the Holiday Gift-Giving Period." Pew Internet & American Life Project. January 23, 2012a. http://www.pewinternet.org/Reports/2012/E-readers-and-tablets/Findings.aspx (accessed January 28, 2012).

Rainie, Lee, Kathryn Zickuhr, Kristen Purcell, Mary Madden, and Joanna Brenner. "The Rise of E-reading." Pew Internet & American Life Project. April 4, 2012b. http://libraries.pewinternet.org/2012/04/04/the-rise-of-e-reading/ (accessed May 19, 2012).

Rao, Leena. "Amazon Kindle Owners Are 'Borrowing' Nearly 300,000 Electronic Books a Month." *TechCrunch*, January 12, 2012. http://techcrunch.com/2012/01/12/amazon-kindle-owners-are-borrowing-nearly-300000-electronic-books-a-month/ (accessed January 29, 2012).

Raphael, Molly. "Ebooks: Promising New Conversations." *E-Content* (blog). *American Libraries*, May 18, 2012. http://americanlibrariesmagazine.org/e-content/ebooks-promising-new-conversations (accessed May 23, 2012).

Rapp, David. "Copyright Clash: Authors Guild and Other Sue HathiTrust and Five Universities." *Library Journal*, September 13, 2011a. http://www.libraryjournal.com/lj/home/892021-264/copyright_clash_authors_guild_and.html.csp (accessed February 5, 2012).

Rapp, David. "Ingram Announces New Library Ebook Access Model and Audiobook Shift." *Library Journal*, April 25, 2011b. http://www.libraryjournal.com/lj/home/890315-264/ingram_announces_new_library_ebook.html.csp (accessed December 18, 2011).

Rich, Motoko. "Literacy Debate: Online, R U Really Reading?" *New York Times*, July 27, 2008. http://www.nytimes.com/2008/07/27/books/27reading.html?pagewanted=all (accessed November 26, 2011).

Richtel, Matt. "A Silicon Valley School That Doesn't Compute." *New York Times*, October 22, 2011. http://www.nytimes.com/2011/10/23/technology/at-waldorf-school-in-silicon-valley-technology-can-wait.html# (accessed November 26, 2011).

Richtel, Matt, and Julie Bosman. "For Their Children, Many E-book Fans Insist on Paper." *New York Times*, November 20, 2011. http://www.nytimes.com/2011/11/21/business/for-their-children-many-e-book-readers-insist-on-paper.html?_r=2&hp (accessed December 28, 2011).

Roberts, Jeff John. "What the eBook Settlement Means for Publishers, Apple and You" *PaidContent*, August 31, 2012. http://paidcontent.org/2012/08/31/explainer-what-the-ebook-settlement-means-for-publishers-apple-and-you/ (accessed September 24, 2012).

Romano, Frank. "E-Books and the Challenge of Preservation." In *Building a National Strategy for Preservation: Issues in Digital Media Archiving*. Washington, DC: Council on Library and Information Resources and the Library of Congress, 2002. http://www.clir.org/pubs/reports/pub106/ebooks.html.

Rosen, Judith. "Two Colorado Libraries Partner with CIPA to Carry E-books." *Publishers Weekly*, March 17, 2011. http://www.publishersweekly.com/pw/by-topic/industry-news/publisher-news/article/46515-two-colorado-libraries-partner-with-cipa-to-carry-e-books.html (accessed December 28, 2011).

Rosenblatt, Bill. "EPUB Lightweight Content Protection: Use Cases & Requirements." International Digital Publishing Forum, May 18, 2012. http://idpf.org/epub-content-protection (accessed September 20, 2012)

Sapieha, Chad. "Review: Homegrown Kobo Hits the Shelves." *Globe and Mail*, April 29, 2012. http://www.theglobeandmail.com/news/technology/gadgets-and-gear/gadgets/review-homegrown-kobo-hits-the-shelves/article1551370/ (accessed January 28, 2012).

Schechner, Karen. "Verso Study Spotlights Consumer Book Buying Behavior." *Bookselling This Week*, February 9, 2012. http://news.bookweb.org/news/verso-study-spotlights-consumer-book-buying-behavior (accessed May 27, 2012).

Schell, Lindsey. "The Academic Library E-book." In *No Shelf Required*, edited by Sue Polanka, 78–93. Chicago: American Library Association, 2011.

Schneider, Karen. "Ebook, Pbooks, Mebooks, and Parrots." *Free Range Librarian*, November 19, 2011. http://freerangelibrarian.com/2011/11/19/ebookpbookmebook/ (accessed December 27, 2011).

Schwartz, Meredith. "Blind Patrons Sue Philly Library for Loaning Inaccessible Nooks." *Library Journal*, May 8, 2012. http://lj.libraryjournal.com/2012/05/industry-news/blind-patrons-sue-philly-library-for-loaning-inaccessible-nooks/ (accessed May 28, 2012).

Schwartz, Meredith. "Penguin, 3M Test Ebook Pilot at NYPL, BPL." *Library Journal*, June 21, 2012. http://lj.libraryjournal.com/2012/06/shows-events/ala/penguin-3m-test-ebook-pilot-at-nypl-bpl/#_ (accessed September 23, 2012).

Sendze, Monique. "The Ebook Evolution: How They'll Change Public Libraries." Presentation at the *Library Journal* Ebook Summit 2011, "Ebooks: The New Normal," October 12, 2011.

Sendze, Monique. Interview by the author. Conference call. February 10, 2012.

"Settlement Agreement." Americans with Disabilities. January 8, 2012. http://www.ada.gov/arizona_state_university.htm (accessed February 4, 2012).

Shank, Jenny. "Pew Survey Shows How E-books Are Changing the Equation for Publisher, Readers." *MediaShift*, April 10, 2012. http://www.pbs.org/mediashift/2012/04/pew-survey-shows-how-e-books-are-changing-the-equation-for-publishers-readers101.html (accessed May 28, 2012).

Shankland, Stephen. "Web-Based Kindle Format Good for Comics, Kids' Books." *CNET*, October 21, 2011. http://news.cnet.com/8301-1001_3-20123608

-92/web-based-kindle-format-good-for-comics-kids-books/ (accessed January 27, 2012).

Shatzkin, Mike. "After the DOJ Action, Where Do We Stand?" *The Shatzkin Files*, April 14, 2012a. http://www.idealog.com/blog/after-the-doj-action-where-do-we-stand/ (accessed May 18, 2012).

Shatzkin, Mike. "The Ebook Marketplace Could Definitely Confuse the Average Consumer." *The Shatzkin Files*, September 17, 2011a. http://www.idealog.com/blog/the-ebook-marketplace-could-definitely-confuse-the-average-consumer (accessed November 12, 2011).

Shatzkin, Mike. "Four Years in to the Ebook Revolution: Things We Know and Things We Don't Know." *The Shatzkin Files*, September 25, 2011b. http://www.idealog.com/blog/four-years-into-the-ebook-revolution-things-we-know-and-things-we-dont-know (accessed January 28, 2012).

Shatzkin, Mike. Interview by author. Phone call November 7, 2011f.

Shatzkin, Mike. "Is an 80% Ebook World for Straight Text Really in Sight?" *The Shatzkin Files*, October 21, 2011c. http://www.idealog.com/blog/is-an-80-ebook-world-for-straight-text-really-in-sight (accessed December 31, 2011).

Shatzkin, Mike. "Letter to the DoJ about the Collusion Lawsuit and Settlement." *The Shatzkin Files*, May 23, 2012b. http://www.idealog.com/blog/letter-to-the-doj-about-the-collusion-lawsuit-and-settlement/ (accessed May 28, 2012).

Shatzkin, Mike. "Remaking an Industry: What Publishers Need to be Thinking about in 2012." *The Shatzkin Files*, January 25, 2012c. http://www.idealog.com/speeches/2012/01/remaking-an-industry/ (accessed January 30, 2012).

Shatzkin, Mike. "Searching for the Formula to Deliver Illustrated Books as Ebooks." *The Shatzkin Files*, November 13, 2011d. http://www.idealog.com/blog/searching-for-the-formula-to-deliver-illustrated-books-as-ebooks (accessed February 5, 2012).

Shatzkin, Mike. "Show Me the Data!" *The Shatzkin Files*, January 16, 2012d. http://www.idealog.com/blog/show-me-the-data (accessed January 28, 2012).

Shatzkin, Mike. "Things Learned and Thoughts Provoked by London Book Fair 2012." *The Shatzkin Files*, April 24, 2012e. http://www.idealog.com/blog/things-learned-and-thoughts-provoked-by-london-book-fair-2012 (accessed April 29, 2012).

Shatzkin, Mike. "Will Book Publishers Be Able to Maintain Primacy as Ebook Publisher?" *The Shatzkin Files*, October 9, 2011e. http://www.idealog.com/blog/will-book-publishers-be-able-to-maintain-primacy-as-ebook-publishers (accessed December 31, 2011).

Sheehan, Kate. "Librarian-Publisher Dialog: Kate Sheehan Talks to Madeline McIntosh of Random House." *Library Journal*, July 21, 2011. http://www.libraryjournal.com/lj/newsletters/newsletterbucketbooksmack/891362-439/librarian-publisher_dialog_kate_sheehan_talks.html.csp (accessed January 29, 2012).

Sirota, David. "Are High-Tech Classrooms Better Classrooms?" *Salon*, February 3, 2012. http://www.salon.com/2012/02/03/are_high_tech_classrooms_better_classrooms/. (accessed February 5, 2012).

"SLJ's 2011 Technology Survey: Things Are Changing. Fast." *School Library Journal*, May 1, 2011. http://www.schoollibraryjournal.com/slj/articlereview/890368-451/ebooks.html.csp (accessed December 28, 2011).

Smith, Mat. "Microsoft Invests $300 Million in New Barnes & Noble 'Strategic Partnership.'" *Engadget*, April 30, 2012. http://www.engadget.com/2012/04/30/microsoft-barnes-and-noble-partnership/ (accessed May 12, 2012).

"Social DRM and Epub." Libreka presentation at the Taiwan Digital Publishing Forum, June 10, 2010. http://www.slideshare.net/taiwandigital/lebrekasocial-drm-and-epub (accessed January 30, 2012).

Spalding, Tim. "Why Are You for Killing Libraries?" *Thingology Blog*, February 5, 2010. http://www.librarything.com/blogs/thingology/2010/02/why-are-you-for-killing-libraries/ (accessed February 5, 2012).

Sporkin, Andi. "Association of American Publishers Endorses United Nations Pilot Project Improving Access to Books Worldwide for the Blind and Visually-Impaired." Association of American Publishers, October 14, 2011. http://www.publishers.org/press/48/ (accessed February 4, 2012).

Stone, Brad. "Amazon Erases Orwell Books from Kindle." *New York Times*, July 17, 2009. http://www.nytimes.com/2009/07/18/technology/companies/18amazon.html (accessed January 28, 2012).

Streitfeld, David. "Amazon Signs Up Authors, Writing Publishers Out of the Deal." *New York Times*, October 16, 2011. http://www.nytimes.com/2011/10/17/technology/amazon-rewrites-the-rules-of-book-publishing.html?_r=1&pagewanted=1 (accessed November 25, 2011).

Tassi, Paul. "You Will Never Kill Piracy and Piracy Will Never Kill You." *Forbes*, February 3, 2012. http://www.forbes.com/sites/insertcoin/2012/02/03/you-will-never-kill-piracy-and-piracy-will-never-kill-you/ (accessed February 4, 2012).

Tate, Ryan. "Amazon Launches Christmas Attack on Local Shops." *Gawker*, December 6, 2011. http://gawker.com/5865612/amazon-launches-christmas-attack-on-local-shops (accessed December 29, 2011).

Thomas, Sue, Chris Joseph, Jess Laccetti, Bruce Mason, Simon Mills, Simon Perril, and Kate Pullinger. "Transliteracy: Crossing Divides." *First Monday* 12, no. 3 (December 2007). http://www.uic.edu/htbin/cgiwrap/bin/ojs/index.php/fm/article/view/2060/1908 (accessed November 26, 2011).

Thompson, John B. *Merchants of Culture: The Publishing Business in the Twenty-First Century*. Malden, MA: Polity Press, 2010.

"TIGAR Objectives and Implementation Strategy." World Intellectual Property Association TIGAR Project. http://www.visionip.org/tigar/en/objectives.html (accessed February 4, 2012).

Titlow, John Paul. "Apple Takes Aim at Education with iBooks 2 and Textbook Publishing Tools." *Read Write Web*, January 18, 2012. http://www.readwriteweb.com/archives/apple_takes_aim_at_textbooks_launches_ibooks_2_and.php (accessed January 29, 2012).

Trubek, Anne. "What Muncie Read." *New York Times*, November 23, 2011. http://www.nytimes.com/2011/11/27/books/review/what-muncie-read.html (accessed December 4, 2011).

Ulanoff, Lance. "This is How Apple Changes Education, Forever" Mashable, January 19, 2012. http://mashable.com/2012/01/19/this-is-how-apple -changes-education-forever/ (accessed September 24, 2012).

Verso Digital. "2011 Survey of Book-Buying Behavior." Presentation at Digital Book World 2012. January 25, 2012. http://www.versoadvertising.com/ DBWsurvey2012/ (accessed January 28, 2012).

"Vision." Gluejar. http://gluejar.com/vision (accessed September 25, 2012).

Walljasper, Jay. *All That We Share: How to Save the Economy, the Environment, the Internet, Democracy, Our Communities and Everything Else That Belongs to All of Us.* New York: The New Press, 2010.

"The Waste Land for iPad." Faber & Faber. June 7, 2011. http://www.faber.co.uk/ article/2011/6/waste-land-ipad-press-release/ (accessed November 26, 2011).

Webb, Jenn. "We're in the Midst of a Restructuring of the Publishing Universe (Don't Panic)." In *Best of TOC 2012*, O'Reilly Team, 11–14. Sebastopol, CA: O'Reilly Media, 2012.

Weinberger, David. "First Build Released." *DPLA Dev*, February 1, 2012. http:// blogs.law.harvard.edu/dplatechdev/2012/02/01/first-build-released/ (accessed February 5, 2012).

Weinberger, David. *Too Big to Know.* New York: Basic Books, 2011.

"Welcome to the Shared Digital Future." HathiTrust. http://www.hathitrust.org/ about (accessed February 5, 2012).

West, Jessamyn. "The Kindle Lending Experience from a Patron's Perspective: 'A Wolf in Book's Clothing.' " *Librarian.net*, November 15, 2011a. http://www .librarian.net/stax/3725/the-kindle-lending-experience-from-a-patrons-perspective -a-wolf-in-books-clothing/ (accessed December 27, 2011).

West, Jessamyn. "Myths about the Digital Divide." Presentation at the CLIR annual meeting, October 12, 2011b. http://www.librarian.net/talks/clir/digdiv.pdf (accessed December 28, 2011).

West, Jessamyn. "Open Library—Making Inroads and Headway in All 50 States." *librarian.net*, November 4, 2011c. http://www.librarian.net/stax/3718/open -library-making-inroads-and-headway-in-all-50-states/ (accessed February 5, 2012).

West, Jessamyn. *Without A Net: Librarians Bridging the Digital Divide.* Santa Barbara, CA: Libraries Unlimited, 2011d.

Whelan, Debra Lau. "More School Libraries Offer Ebooks; Increased Demand, Rise in Circulation," *School Library Journal*, October 13, 2011. http://www .schoollibraryjournal.com/slj/home/892394-312/more_school_libraries_offer _ebooks.html.csp (accessed May 28, 2012).

Williams, Christopher. "E-books Drive Older Women to Digital Piracy." *Telegraph*, May 17, 2011. http://www.telegraph.co.uk/technology/news/8518755/ E-books-drive-older-women-to-digital-piracy.html (accessed January 8, 2012).

Windows Dev Center. "XML Paper Specification: Overview." http://msdn.microsoft .com/en-us/windows/hardware/gg463373 (accessed January 27, 2012).

Wineman, Dan. "Common Misconceptions about What I Wrote Yesterday." *Venomous Porridge*, January 20, 2012. http://venomousporridge.com/post/ 16178567783/common-misconceptions (accessed January 29, 2012).

Wohl, Jessica, "Wal-mart Stops Selling Amazon Kindles." Reuters, September 20, 2012. http://www.reuters.com/article/2012/09/20/us-walmart-amazon -kindle-idUSBRE88J0WA20120920 (accessed September 26, 2012).

Worona, Steve. "Naughty Bit." *EDUCAUSE Review* 42, no. 4 (July/August 2007): 70–71. http://www.educause.edu/EDUCAUSE+Review/EDUCAUSEReview MagazineVolume42/NaughtyBit/161755 (accessed May 12, 2012).

Yelton, Andromeda. "Ebooks Choices and the Soul of Librarianship." *The Digital Shift*, July 30, 2012. http://www.thedigitalshift.com/2012/07/ebooks/ ebooks-choices-and-the-soul-of-librarianship/ (accessed September 24, 2012).

Yelton, Andromeda. Interview by the author. Skype. November 9, 2011.

Zickuhr, Kathryn, Lee Rainie, Kristen Purcell, Mary Madden, and Joanna Brenner. "Libraries, Patrons, and Ebooks." Pew Internet & American Life Project. June 22, 2012. http://libraries.pewinternet.org/2012/06/22/libraries-patrons -and-e-books/ (accessed July 9, 2012).

Zimmer, Carl. "The Brain: How Google Is Making Us Smarter." *Discover Magazine*. January 15, 2009. http://discovermagazine.com/2009/feb/15-how-google-is -making-us-smarter/article_view?b_start:int=0&-C= (accessed September 2, 2012).

INDEX

About the Author

KATE SHEEHAN is the special projects coordinator for Bibliomation, a consortium of public and school libraries in Connecticut. She joined Bibliomation in 2009 to work on their migration to the Evergreen ILS as the open source implementation coordinator and has been fortunate that the good people of Bibliomation have been willing to scrape together funding to keep her popping up at meetings. Kate has been the coordinator of knowledge and learning services at Darien Library and the coordinator of library automation at Danbury Public Library, which was the first library to implement LibraryThing for Libraries. Prior to joining Danbury Public Library, she was a technology and reference librarian at the Ferguson Library in Stamford, Connecticut. A graduate of Smith College, Kate's post-college experiences in the corporate workplace inspired her decision to get an MSLIS from Simmons. She finished library school in December of 2003 and has been happily ensconced in the public library sphere since then. When she's not coordinating, she works as a writer and consultant and blogs at loosecannonlibrarian.net and ALA TechSource.

CPSIA information can be obtained at www.ICGtesting.com
Printed in the USA
LVOW10s1911180314

377915LV00003B/73/P